ANIMAL RIGHTS

ANIMAL RIGHTS

STORIES OF PEOPLE WHO DEFEND THE RIGHTS OF ANIMALS

By Patricia Curtis

FOUR WINDS PRESS
NEW YORK

PICTURE CREDITS

Paul Duckworth/A.S.P.C.A., 20; Dr. Michael W. Fox/H.S.U.S., 72; Humane Society of the United States, 34; Gavin Mather/DPI, 90; Joe Munroe/Photo Researchers, xii; Dick Randall/© 1979 Defenders of Wildlife, 50; Arthur Schatz/Life Magazine © 1968 Time, Inc., 108; Lanna Peyton Swindler/H.S.U.S., 128.

LIBRARY OF CONGRESS CATALOGING IN PUBLICATION DATA

Curtis, Patricia.
Animal rights.

Bibliography: p.
SUMMARY: Focuses on seven individuals who are working to defend and extend the rights of animals including pets, wild animals, zoo animals, laboratory animals, and others.
 1. Animals, Treatment of—United States—Juvenile literature. 2. Animals, Treatment of—Law and legislation—United States—Juvenile literature.
[1. Animals—Treatment. 2. Animals—Treatment—Law and legislation] I. Title.
HV4725.U33C87   179'.3'0973   79-22451
ISBN 0-590-07650-7

Published by Four Winds Press
A division of Scholastic Magazines, Inc., New York, N.Y.
Copyright © 1980 by Patricia Curtis
All rights reserved
Printed in the United States of America
Library of Congress Catalog Card Number: 79-22451
1 2 3 4 5 84 83 82 81 80

Acknowledgments

In expressing my appreciation to the people who helped me, I must mention Jean Stewart first of all. Her good judgment, wide knowledge, and unflagging encouragement were invaluable to me. I was also fortunate in having David Reuther for my editor and came to rely greatly on his trustworthy guidance and consistent support.

My warm thanks go to Dr. Michael W. Fox; Henry Mark Holzer; Dr. Dallas Pratt of Argus Archives; Peter Batten; Dr. John McArdle; Elinor Molbegott; Eric Plasa; Joan R. Blue; Roland C. Clement; Dr. Frank M. Loew; Robbins Barstow of the Connecticut Cetacean Society; Jim Mason; Barbara Thomson; Bianca Beary; Kathy Savesky; Helen Jones; Devon Griffiths; and William W. Davis.

I also wish to thank Dr. Stephen R. Kellert, who gave me valuable background material, and the professors of philosophy who generously sent me information and talked with me about the basic concept of the rights of animals: Professors Lawrence C. Becker, Thomas L. Benson, Sidney Gendin, Fred Hombach, Dale Jamieson, Michael Martin, James Otten, James Rachels, Tom Regan, Lilly-Marlene Russow, Tom Simon, and Bonnie Steinbock.

And I acknowledge with gratitude and affection the help of Dorothy Glasser and Rachel Paine, who typed—and typed and typed.

—Patricia Curtis

THE animal defenders who tell their stories in this book are all fictional people, but their experiences and observations are based on true events or authentic situations.

CONTENTS

    Foreword by Dr. Michael W. Fox   *ix*
1 • Of Mice and Men: Laboratory Animal
    Experimentation   *1*
2 • Raining Cats and Dogs: The Treatment of Pets   *21*
3   Peaceable Giants: The Extinction of Whales
    and Dolphins   *35*
4 • Whose Wildlife? Hunting and Trapping   *51*
5 • We Are What We Eat: Factory Farming   *73*
6 • Prisons or Havens? A Look at Zoos   *91*
7 • Ride 'Em, Cowboy! The Use of Animals for
    Entertainment   *109*
8 • Animal Rights   *129*
    Further Reading   *140*
    Organizations   *145*

Foreword

The battle for human rights has a long and continuing history from the abolition of slavery and child labor to the equal rights amendment. In the wake of battles against racism and sexism, the fight against "speciesism" —the belief that animals are subhuman, unfeeling machines that are here to serve mankind exclusively—is just beginning. While humane societies have been fighting cruelty and other abuses of animals for decades, the animal rights movement is an entirely new dimension of this struggle.

When we speak of animal rights, we imply that we have certain duties toward animals. As Patricia Curtis shows in the eight chapters in this book, there is a great need for consciousness raising to elevate the relationship of human beings with animals from one of utilitarian exploitation to one of compassionate, humane stewardship. Look beneath the many abuses of animals that are described here. These are the surface symptoms of a deeper set of values and attitudes toward nonhuman life which need to be changed for the betterment of society and all life on earth.

How can these values and attitudes be changed? First, by recognizing that animals are entitled to certain rights and second, even though it hurts, by accepting the fact that the abuse and exploitation of animals described in his book are taking place this very day.

Just before I sat down to write this foreword, I came across a scientific article recently published by a team of animal scientists who were reporting their findings on the effects of malnutrition on the development of fetal pigs. In their experiment, pregnant sows were deprived of all food for as long as forty days—forty days and nights of starvation. Surely no matter how "significant" the data might be from such an experiment, there should be certain limits as to what one can or cannot do to an animal in the search for knowledge. This kind of experimentation transcends all limits.

Education and protective legislation are two important keys to protecting the rights of animals. The point has now come where it is socially and ecologically imperative for people to develop moral codes and laws to protect plant and animal species and the environment as a whole from further human depredation and destruction. At one time, women, children, prisoners and slaves had no rights. In most "civilized" countries, they now do have rights—and as we become more civilized, animals and all things of nature will fall, not under our dominion, but within the scope of our moral concern.

From a strictly utilitarian view, respect for human rights can mean a better society for humankind. Recognition of animal rights can help expand our traditionally human-centered view, and could mean a better world for all people and animals alike. As Mahatma Gandhi observed, "The greatness of a nation and its moral progress can be judged by the way its animals are treated."

The time to recognize and respect animal rights has come. We need veterinarians, ethologists and humane educators who can speak for the health and husbandry requirements of animals and define their basic needs and

Foreword

rights. They may do much to promote a deeper understanding of animals and responsible compassion in our relationships with them. This book is also of great value in this regard. It will undoubtedly be a source of lively classroom debate and should do more than merely sensitize young adults to the plights and rights of animals. It exposes them to those values and attitudes associated with our regard for and treatment of animals. The ethical questions that arise will be of immense educational value and will, it is hoped, extend beyond the classroom to improve the welfare of animals under humankind's careful stewardship.

Director
The Institute for the
   Study of Animal Problems

Michael W. Fox, D.Sc., Ph.D.,
B. Vet. Med., M.R.C.V.S.

1

OF MICE AND MEN:
Laboratory Animal Experimentation

*Bill Davidson, who tells this story,
is a first-year medical student.*

WHEN I was in eighth grade, I became aware that I was going to have a problem in my biology class. I knew from my friends in the grade ahead of me that this was the class in which the students would be dissecting frogs and mice.

Already my class had participated in a number of experiments that had made me very uncomfortable. The kids had brought in living butterflies, moths, and other insects, which they had chloroformed and taken apart. They had dropped acid on earthworms and watched the creatures squirm, curl, and die. Once in class the teacher had placed frogs in ice water to observe the way the animals' breathing and movements slowed down; I remember thinking that it was mean, and I couldn't see what additional knowledge we had gained from watching the actual process.

A ninth-grade boy had conducted an experiment on his own and won a prize for it at a science fair. Over a period of months he had systematically smothered several dozen mice by placing plastic bags over their heads on the outlandish theory that he could breed a line of mice that could learn to breathe through their skin. He mounted photographs of the dead subjects and wrote a report on them. The judges praised the boy for his enterprise. Another kid had attempted heart transplants with two unanesthetized pet rabbits; and one student had blinded some pigeons, also without anesthetic, to see if they could fly without their sight. I was sickened by all of it. I felt there was something very wrong, but at the time I couldn't figure out how to make an effective protest.

I was a pretty good student, a member of the basketball team, and editor of the school paper. I had many good friends, and in general was happy in school. But what I loved most of all was spending time with my animals at home. I had two dogs, three cats, and a nanny goat I had raised myself. I had rabbits, hamsters, rats, guinea pigs, an iguana, a parakeet, and even a small snake in a terrarium. I took good care of my pets, and at that time I planned to go into some kind of work with animals when I grew up—as a veterinarian, perhaps, or zoo director, or maybe working in animal protection. That was before I decided to become a doctor, but I think wanting to help people is connected to my affection for animals—I see it as part of the same feeling.

Anyway, I felt that the "work" the class was about to do with the frogs and mice was unnecessary and cruel.

"I think it's dumb," I said to my friend Michael one day. "We've seen the insides of frogs and mice in the pictures in our textbook and in slides the teacher showed us in class."

Michael didn't like the idea either. "But what can we do? If we don't go along, Mr. Harris will flunk us," he pointed out.

I also mentioned my feelings to Emily, a girl in my class. "Oh, I don't intend to take part in that at all—I'm going to say it makes me sick," she said. "Harris always lets girls leave the room if they want to—he's real old-fashioned that way. I don't like to get out of things because I'm a girl, but in this case I think I'll take advantage of it."

The more I thought about it, the more objectionable the animal experiments seemed to me. One night at dinner I told my parents. They listened and didn't say anything for a little while. Then my mother said, "Bill, if you really feel strongly about this—and I can see you do—why don't you ask to speak privately to Mr. Harris and tell him? I think you have a good point."

And my father said, "Why don't you also offer to do some other kind of biology experiment that doesn't involve animals and see if he'll accept that instead? Or you might suggest an experiment with an animal that won't hurt it—construct a maze and make a behavior study with one of your guinea pigs, or make a detailed observation of the habits of some animals in the woods."

But when I approached Mr. Harris, he reacted with annoyance. He said he had many classes to teach, papers to grade; he seemed to feel my idea would make more work for him. He explained he had a course plan or syllabus to follow that called for dissecting frogs and mice, and his classes had always done it. I got the idea that he felt if he allowed a student to get out of it, he would have to explain why to the higher-ups in the school, and he had enough problems without attracting more. He turned down my proposal.

My parents and I discussed the situation together. Finally my father said, "Bill, if you want to take a stand on this and refuse to do the experiments, we'll back you. And if you are flunked for not performing them, we'll help you make a case before the school authorities. I think there's a principle involved here that's larger than the matter of class participation."

When the other students heard what I was doing, several of them decided to join me. Michael wanted to, but his parents were unsympathetic and threatened to punish him if he "made trouble" at school. Emily decided she would rather take my position instead of copping out, as she put it, on the basis of being a girl. She and Howard, Sharon, Amy, and Jonathan helped me draw up a petition to the principal of our school.

The principal, Mr. Ungar, was a young man who everybody knew had ambitions for advancing in the education system of the county and even the state. He liked to think of his school as progressive and democratic. He discussed our petition with his assistant principal, Mrs. Rosenberg. He listened to Mr. Harris. I'm sure he was not unmindful of the stir the controversy would surely cause in the PTA and the school board. Mr. Ungar sincerely wanted to be fair, but he also wanted to do the up-and-coming thing.

While he was deliberating the best way to handle the situation, a local newspaper ran a story about it. The writer of the article was highly sympathetic to our position, and made a point about our right to respect life in all its various forms. The article said that public opinion was beginning to change toward the use of animals in classrooms. It also pointed out examples of an increasingly negative attitude on the part of many people toward the use of animals for many kinds of tests in research laboratories.

Mr. Ungar decided that the progressive thing to do was to grant our petition. He diplomatically praised Mr. Harris for his dedication to duty but asked him to think up some creative alternate experiments for us to conduct.

So several helpless frogs and mice were spared in the eighth-grade biology class of one school, and I learned a valuable lesson in dissent.

I didn't know it then, but the issues we raised are important ones, far larger than our personal feelings and the tradition followed by our teacher. Today in the United States between 60 and 90 million mice, rats, guinea pigs, hamsters, dogs, cats, rabbits, monkeys—even ponies, cows, calves, sheep, pigs, and birds—are killed every year in experimental research in the laboratories of universities, medical centers, drug companies, cosmetic companies, and chemical manufacturers. The animals are presumably sacrificed to test the safety and efficiency of products and procedures for human beings, to help understand human biology and behavior, and to make life more comfortable for people. Scientists say they use animals for these tests because animals are so *similar* to human beings in their life systems. At the same time, they justify their use of animals because they say animals are so *different* from human beings in their capacity to suffer and in their importance in the scheme of things.

There is no question that in the past many medical discoveries were made possible by animal research. Unfortunately, most of these advances made billions of animals suffer terribly. And most of the research conducted today involves fear, pain, and death for those millions of animals that are used every year.

Most research scientists insist that the use of animals is necessary, and they discourage the public from questioning what they do because they believe it is impossible for nonscientists to understand its necessity and value. They also feel that experimentation doesn't even have to have any direct application to human betterment; they contend that scientific curiosity and investigation are enough to justify it. In that respect, they are like many biology teachers and science-fair judges.

Researchers also point out that some experimentation is directed toward the betterment of animals. Advances in veterinary medicine and the care of domestic animals have come about through animal research. But this work represents a very, very small part of the total amount of animal research, even though a little of it does benefit other animals.

Most folks don't have the faintest idea of what goes on in animal research laboratories, and prefer not to know. It upsets them to hear of animals being made to suffer, but they believe it is necessary for scientific progress. They are intimidated by the research scientists and feel unequipped to criticize them. And the public is justifiably frightened by mysterious diseases such as cancer, and believes that the search for its cure is what animal research is all about. I thought a lot about these things myself when I was deciding to become a scientist.

Of Mice and Men: Laboratory Animal Experimentation

To give you just a minimal idea of how some animals are used in research laboratories:

Over 100,000 dogs a year are subjected to tests involving radiation, poisons, viruses, electric shock, drug addiction, stress, and surgical experiments such as organ transplants. They are subjected to battering tests in which their legs or other parts of their bodies are given repeated blows with hammers so that researchers can study the bruises and broken bones. In some labs, dogs are treated upon arrival to a neat little piece of surgery that destroys their vocal cords so they can't bark or whine.

Dogs have also been used in some particularly vicious tests called "learned helplessness." One group of dogs is subjected to painful electric shocks in a cage until in their agitation they accidentally scramble over a barrier and get away from the shocks. Another group of dogs is made to endure two series of shocks—the first administered to them while they are restrained. When these dogs are then put in the cage where the other dogs escaped, they just whimper and make no effort to get away from the second series of painful shocks—establishing for the researchers' satisfaction that they have learned to be helpless.

Cats and kittens are used for tests involving stress, electric shock, nerve damage, viruses, and poisons. They are subjected to intense heat to see how much they can endure before dying. Would you believe cats are even made to become alcoholics and forced to endure alcoholism tests?

Many types of monkeys are preferred for tests in which they are totally immobilized for weeks and even months and then "terminated" so the effects of restraint on their internal organs can be studied. With electrodes planted in their brains, they are examined in endless behavior studies. Baboons have been used in automobile-crash experiments in which they are hurled against simulated dashboards; pregnant baboons have been used in crash tests to determine the efficiency of seat belts. Monkeys are forced to become drug addicts and then forced into withdrawal. And they are still to this day made to inhale cigarette smoke, as if years of studying human lungs had told us nothing.

Worst of all, I think, are the radiation experiments that monkeys have been subjected to at the Armed Forces Radiobiology Research Institute. The tests involve teaching these smart animals to avoid painful electric shocks, subjecting them to radiation, and then observing their shock-avoiding ability after radiation, with the poor animals vomiting and sick, until they die. Thousands of monkeys have been tortured this way—and as far as I know it's still going on.

About ten years ago a scientist named Harry Harlow became famous for his studies in which he took baby monkeys away from their mothers and raised them in boxes without any contact with other monkeys or human beings. The babies grew up anxious, neurotic, and severely depressed. He gave other infant monkeys mechanical "monster mothers," made out of terrycloth and wire, that subjected the babies to different sorts of very cruel treatment. For example, one monster mother heated up till it burned the baby clinging to it. Harlow said his work with these monkeys proved many theories about the effects on human babies of being deprived of their mothers or of having cruel mothers.

Rabbits are particularly used in tests aimed at determining whether or not substances are harmful to the human eye. Rabbits' eyes don't form tears to wash out irritants as efficiently as ours do, and so their eyes are particularly susceptible to pain, damage, and blindness. Cosmetic companies test mascara and other eye makeup on rabbits. Other companies that make aerosol compounds use rabbits for the same reasons; the chemicals are sprayed into the rabbits' eyes until they cause the eyes to hemorrhage, or the animals are forced to breathe noxious aerosol fumes until they sicken or die.

About 75 percent of all animals used in labs for any purposes are rats and mice. These animals are practical for research because they are small, easy to handle, and they breed rapidly, yet as mammals they are assumed to be sufficiently like human beings in their life processes to make research with them meaningful. Unfortunately for rats and mice, the public is for the most part indifferent about their being used in laboratories. If people learned that cute little puppies were subjected to tests in which 30 percent of their body was badly burned, or in which they were given repeated electric shocks until they died, people would be very upset and raise a great protest. But the same folks can hear about the same tests being made on rats and mice and shrug it off.

Almost as long as animal experimentation has been going on in research laboratories, there have been people who have objected to it. In England and America, groups calling themselves antivivisectionists—*vivi* meaning "alive," *sect* meaning "to cut"—were formed in the nineteenth century and protested animal experimentation. As long ago as 1876, England passed the Cruelty to Animals

Act, which gives some protection to lab animals. It does not set limitations on research but mandates certain humane standards of care. Our country didn't consider the treatment of lab animals important enough for legislation until 1966. Our law, the Animal Welfare Act, came into being partly because of the horrible conditions found among the dealers who supply animals to the labs—and the conditions under which the animals were housed and fed in laboratories themselves. The law was broadened a bit in 1970 and 1978 to require the licensing of zoos, circuses, etc., and to give protection to more types of animals.

Unfortunately, while the Animal Welfare Act is better than nothing, it has some big loopholes. First, the act applies to only about 4 percent of the animals used in laboratories (rather a big loophole). While dogs, cats, primates, rabbits, hamsters, and guinea pigs are covered, mice and rats—which make up the majority—are specifically excluded. Second, the law does not limit the cruelty of experiments that may be performed—it is directed mainly at the housing and care of lab animals. Third, while on the one hand the act mandates the use of pain relievers for animals that are made to suffer, on the other hand it exempts researchers from using pain relievers if they say that pain is a necessary part of the experiments. For instance, if a substance administered to an animal is poisonous or severely irritating, the researcher may state that being able to observe pain is essential. Electric shock or burn tests are typical experiments in which pain killers are withheld. There is even a test, called the "writhing test," intended to assess the potential of pain-relieving drugs. Irritants are injected into the stomachs of rats and mice until they writhe in pain; their agony is part of the experiment. When I read about the writhing test and thought about the rats I had as a boy, and how cute and smart they were, I was outraged.

There is no evidence that rats and mice suffer any less than dogs, cats, monkeys, or even human beings do. There are apparently great differences in intelligence among animals; we are only beginning to understand how animals think, acquire information, and use knowledge. But according to some scientific findings, all vertebrates (animals with backbones) feel pain to much the same degree.

Another loophole is that emotional pain is not even mentioned in the Animal Welfare Act. Animals exhibit pain, both physical and emotional, differently. While dogs whine and yelp, cats may suffer in stoic silence. A monkey who is crouched, motionless, in a corner of its cage is undoubtedly in severe emotional pain—but it is not protected by the act. It has been shown that substantial numbers of dogs and cats die in lab cages during the weeks they are being made ready for research. Some were once family pets who were kidnapped for labs or turned over to labs by shelters. They die simply from fear and depression, or from diseases they already had which worsened because of their fear and depression.

The National Institutes of Health, which awards vast sums of money every year for experiments that use animals, have issued guidelines for researchers working with NIH grants. Like the Animal Welfare Act, these guidelines or recommendations are mainly aimed at keeping lab animals more comfortable in their cages. The

Food and Drug Administration has also set certain standards for animal studies at the laboratories it regulates. If researchers choose to follow these recommendations, lab animals in many places will suffer somewhat less.

Today, thanks to the work of the humane groups, there is an awakening concern for laboratory animals. Books and magazine articles, films and TV programs are making people aware of animal experimentation who never thought much or knew about it before.

I spent my junior year of college at a university in London, and by chance, because of my love of animals, I got to know quite a few people who were involved in animal welfare. In spite of the fact that fox hunting is still a popular sport there, England has a strong humane movement. One friend of mine, a fellow student, even let me come along with him and a group of his activist friends on an unusual adventure one night—at least it was unusual for me. I'll never forget it.

A group of about ten of us drove in several cars to an animal laboratory attached to a large chemical company in North London. We parked on the deserted side streets and approached the factory. It was a dark night with clouds scurrying across the moon. We all wore very dark clothes. Through the lighted window we saw the night watchman check the door leading from the lab to the factory; it seemed firmly locked, and he went on his way toward the other end of the buildings.

As soon as he had been gone for a short time, four of us ran up the driveway that led directly to the lab. Around the building we went and hoisted my friend, who was a small guy, up to the sill of a partly open window. In

Of Mice and Men: Laboratory Animal Experimentation 13

he went, and quickly opened the outside door, taking care not to make noise.

As we entered, some of the dogs in the cages began to whine and bark.

"Shh, there, there, quiet now," somebody whispered. We worked swiftly, unlocking cages. Our hearts were really pounding. Arms full of wiggling, ecstatic puppies, we ran to the door and handed the dogs out to other silent figures who had followed us in the shadows.

"Remember, now, take only the pups," whispered the leader. "We can't help these other poor suffering blighters." He indicated other animals, bandaged and silent, lying in the cages.

Nevertheless, one young woman quickly scooped up a young cat that was desperately reaching its paws through the mesh of its cage. She caught up with the rest of us, and we left as quickly and quietly as we had come.

Next day, one of the group phoned a London newspaper. "This is the Animal Liberation Front," he said. "We have taken eleven beagle pups that were scheduled for cigarette-smoking experiments at Empire Chemical. We plan to continue this kind of direct action until all needless animal experimentation is ended."

We had also helped ourselves to a handful of Empire Chemical's files—papers describing some of their experiments. We dropped those in the mail to the newspaper, which made good use of them in the story it ran about our raid.

Of course, we placed the beagle pups in prearranged homes outside of London. The girl who took the cat kept it.

The Animal Liberation Front has been carrying out

commando-style raids like this one for many years. The members have never harmed any people and have saved a good many animals. Occasionally some of the members are caught, arrested, and serve prison sentences. They say their goal is to dramatize the extent and the types of experimentation on animals and the need to drastically reduce them. Truthfully, they have not made a dent in the large, entrenched organizations that conduct research, but they have made a lot of Britons think. They represent a gut reaction to animal experimentation that many people can relate to. I would have enjoyed going on more raids, but I was afraid that, as a foreigner, if I were caught I'd be deported, and it would mess up my schooling. But I did whatever I could with the ALF—I liked them for their spirit. So do many Britons.

Recently some people calling themselves the Animal Liberation Front conducted a raid at New York University Medical Center to call attention to animal research there. Three women and a man dressed in white smocks and posing as professors got into the research laboratory and casually walked off with two dogs, two guinea pigs, and a cat. The cat had electrodes attached to its skull. I heard that the next day a sympathetic veterinarian removed the electrodes and asked no questions.

One of the university's scientists got on television and made a big speech about how the Animal Liberation Front had dealt a blow to cancer research. I think his statement was just "show biz," using the public's fear of cancer to make the ALF look bad. My impression, however, is that most people reacted sympathetically to the ALF's dramatic stunt, although there are people who are

Of Mice and Men: Laboratory Animal Experimentation 15

turned off by this extreme (and illegal) activism.

The question of whether or not research on living animals is justified is a very difficult one for me. In fact, there is no single question—there are many. Is experimentation okay on rats and mice, simply because they are less attractive than puppies and kittens? Is research directly aimed at curing cancer justifiable, but not cruel behavior research such as the learned helplessness tests? For that matter, can the behavior of stressed captive animals teach us about human nature at all? Is it one thing to try out new techniques of, say, open-heart surgery on dogs before they are used on people, but something else altogether to hurt and blind rabbits so that a new mascara can be put on the market? Must the same tests go on at a dozen different research centers, torturing a million animals for essentially the same results? Finally, are there practical alternatives to the use of living animals that researchers could use instead? And since a great deal of medical research with animals is funded by taxpayers' money, shouldn't the public have a say in it?

Many people think the best answers lie in the development of alternative research methods. There are at least two organizations in England and one in our country that fund scientists to conduct research aimed at discovering and developing substitutes for animals. Some of this money has already produced methods that spare animals. One grant from the American Fund for Alternatives to Animal Research went to a West Coast biology professor to perfect a very important test that determines whether or not a substance will cause birth defects. In the past, it was necessary to use pregnant animals for this test. The professor has figured out a way to get accurate results more quickly and inexpensively by using certain one-celled organisms instead.

Along with the English and American organizations, there is the International Association Against Painful Experiments on Animals, which has groups in thirty-nine countries. It is good to think that virtually all over the world there are people who are trying to turn research away from the use of animals and toward other methods. And many humane groups here say that our government, which spends billions of dollars every year in grants for research using animals, should fund the development of alternative testing methods instead. Perhaps I will go into this kind of work as a doctor, though I think I'd rather be involved with treating patients.

What are other possible alternatives to animals? One, developed by a California biochemist named Bruce Ames, uses bacteria instead of animals to determine whether or not a chemical can cause cancer. Then, there has been much success in growing viruses in egg embryos. Tissue cultures are another promising substitute. Certainly the use of human tissues and organs from hospital operating rooms and autopsy rooms could serve in place of animals in many instances. Computers could be used to store information, analyze data, and even predict the properties of new drugs. Computers can even be programmed to simulate living animals. Models could replace animals in classrooms—models have already replaced monkeys in auto-crash tests.

Many alternatives to animals that are already in use were discovered by scientists who were not necessarily looking for ways to spare animals but for quicker and more accurate tests. The idea of substitutes for animals is not a far-out notion. Substitutes are discovered and put into use all the time; the point is that many, many more are needed. And unfortunately many alternative tests are still regarded as additions to animal tests, rather than as substitutes.

Perhaps if the medical profession were more open-minded about accepting the results of other types of research and information from other professions, it wouldn't be necessary to conduct experiments with animals to discover what other professionals already know. For example, virtually everything Professor Harlow claimed he proved in his cruel work with the baby monkeys was already known to psychologists and social workers who dealt with human infants. Since Harlow's tests with monkeys were presumably supposed to help us to understand human babies, I wonder why this particular type of experiment was considered by doctors to be such a breakthrough.

A British physiologist, D. H. Smyth, recently made a thorough study of all the presently existing alternatives to animals, and concluded that it was unrealistic to expect that the complete phasing out of animal experimentation will happen soon. There are not yet enough reliable alternatives, and some experiments—types of surgery, for example—will be especially difficult to replace. But Dr. Smyth admits that his report has not dealt at all with the moral considerations and suggests that objections on humane grounds may be justified. "Everyone has a right to decide that certain procedures are unacceptable," he says.

"Some knowledge can be obtained at too high a price."

One area under reconsideration by scientists as well as humanitarians is the use of animals by students in classrooms and in science fairs. Soon after my experience in eighth grade, I heard that many science educators are beginning to reject the idea that anything goes in the name of scientific investigation by students. They point out that many horrible experiments are performed by youngsters with lots of curiosity but insufficient knowledge and information to realize the cruelty, hopelessness, and absurdity of what they are doing. Such experiments are condemned by scientists who respect life and understand research. And in fact, there seems to be a growing movement to limit student use of living animals in classrooms. California, Illinois, Maine, Connecticut, Pennsylvania, and Massachusetts have recently passed laws to this effect. Canada has ruled out the use of animals in science fairs, unless the projects are harmless observations of the normal living patterns of wild animals, pets, or domestic animals.

Very soon I will face a difficult time in my training. Although it is a routine part of any doctor's education, I do not intend to perform any experiments on living vertebrate animals. I'm working to become a top student because, among other reasons, I will then be in a stronger position when and if the time comes that I will refuse to do certain work. I've read that recently several hundred medical students in Holland refused to kill animals; some have managed to get all the way through medical school and graduate without performing any vivisections. I hope I can do the same.

Reducing the suffering of laboratory animals is one thing; dealing with the question of our right to use animals for experimentation is another. People justify it because human beings are the dominant species—the "tyrant species," some philosophers call us. In that sense, we assume that our species is superior and therefore we are entitled to use other species in any way we choose.

Today we read with disgust and horror about some of the customs that human beings practiced in the past without thinking anything about it at the time—human sacrifice, slavery, public torture and execution, child labor, and the like. Some people say that future generations will look at what we do to animals in laboratories with the same wonder and repugnance. And other people think that experiments with animals can all too easily lead to the use of human beings for the same purposes, as happened under the Nazis.

Richard Ryder, a British psychologist and writer on animal welfare, points out that until recently it was thought that the major factors separating human beings from animals were our development of language and our use of tools. Today we know that some animals make and use tools and some can be taught language. Suppose, asks Ryder, we discovered wild human beings who had no language and had not developed tools—would we be justified in putting them in laboratories and conducting experiments on them? Or suppose some vastly intelligent creatures from outer space came to earth—would they be justified in using us for experiments?

That's something to think about, isn't it?

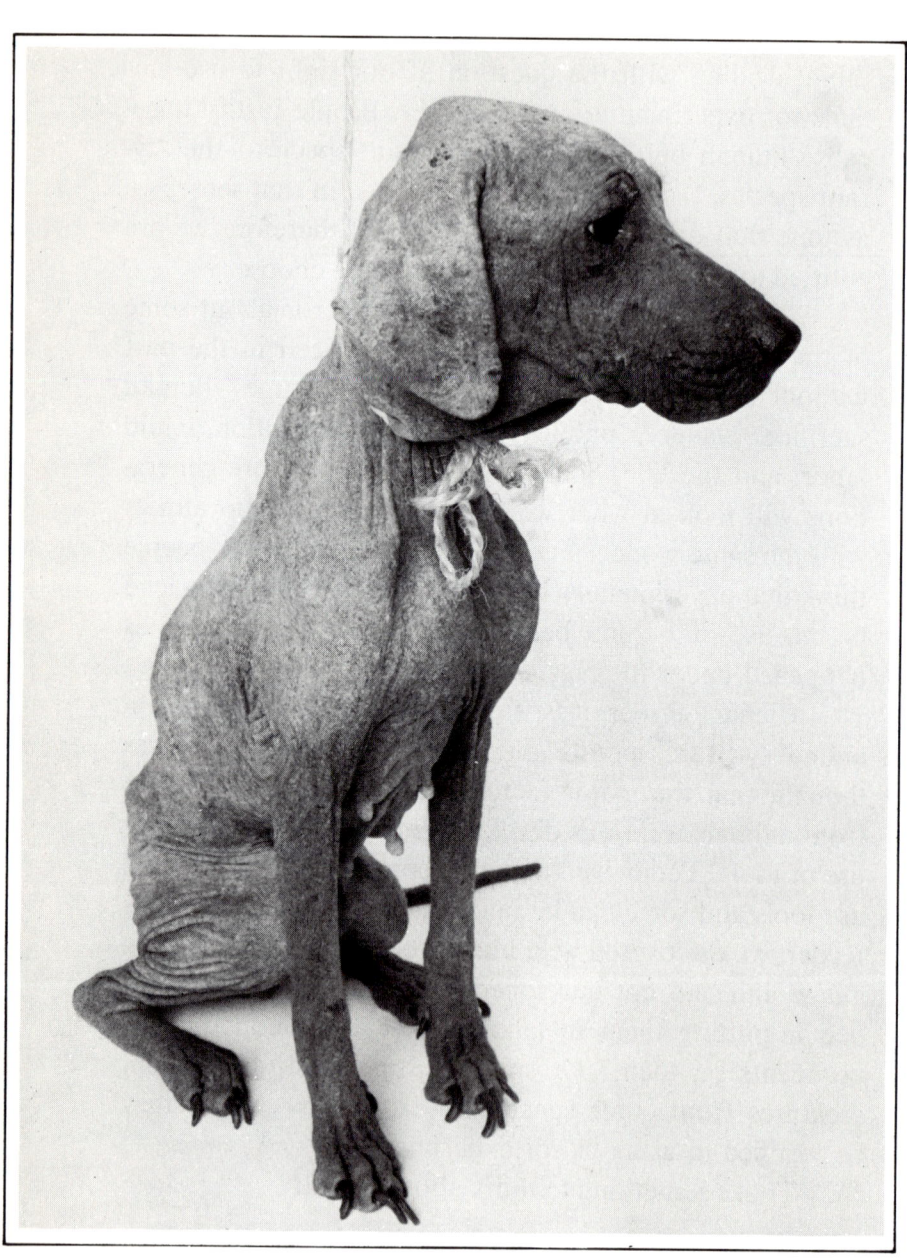

2

RAINING CATS AND DOGS: The Treatment of Pets

***Barbara Hall is a lawyer
for a humane organization.***

ONE day at headquarters we received a phone call from an indignant young woman. "I just saw somebody toss a cat out of a car on the highway," she said. "Isn't that against the law? Can you people do anything about it?"

Our switchboard operator connected her to the department that investigates and handles such complaints.

"Indeed we can," said Ernie, one of our investigators, "if you got the license number of the car."

"Yes, I was driving right behind—I got the license, but by the time I could turn off the highway and drive back to where they threw out the cat, I couldn't find it. It must have gotten away. I don't think it was hit by a car because I didn't see its body."

"We'll go out and try to find the cat," Ernie promised, "but let me have the license number. It was fast thinking on your part to get it."

Fortunately it was a license from our state, which

made it easier to find the person who abandoned the cat. Ernie also took down the young woman's name, which was Judith Sullivan, her address and telephone number, and noted the location where she saw the incident. The chances of finding the cat were not great, but he would give it a try.

Ernie spent a couple of hours driving around the area asking people if they had seen such a cat, but no luck. However, a few days later, we got a call from some people who lived not far from the spot, saying their dog had treed a cat they thought must be a stray, and they couldn't get it down from the tree, it was so badly frightened. One of our people went and got it and brought it to the shelter. It was a gray female who had had kittens recently and whose footpads were badly scraped as though she had been thrown onto pavement. Judith Sullivan had told us she thought it was a gray cat she had seen tossed from the moving car.

Meanwhile, I had gotten into the act. I'm Barbara Hall, the staff attorney for a humane society that has legal status within our state to enforce the animal welfare laws and prosecute animal abuse cases. Abandonment is a form of abuse, although many people don't realize it.

All states have anticruelty laws and a state or city agency that tries to enforce them. But each agency needs the cooperation of the public to report cases and help get the laws enforced. That's why we were so glad that Judith Sullivan had gotten that license number, called us, and said she would be willing to testify in court if necessary.

I traced the license through the Motor Vehicle Bureau and found out who the owner of the car was. We issued a summons for him to appear in court. When the case came up, Judith Sullivan came to court and told the judge what she had seen.

What was interesting was the man's reaction to being brought into criminal court. He was thunderstruck by the idea that he had done something illegal by throwing out his own cat.

"I could have taken her to a shelter, but my wife said no, they always kill them at the shelters," he explained. "So we decided to give her her freedom instead. My wife and kids were in the car. We just slowed down and tossed her out into the bushes beside the road. We figured she'd run away from the highway and not get hit. Some people throw their animals out on the road so they'll get killed by cars behind them—we would never do that, no sir!"

"Why did you want to get rid of your pet?" I asked.

"We got her as a kitten, but when she grew up she ran out of the house and got pregnant. We decided to let her have one litter, for the children, y'know, so they could see the miracle of birth. But we couldn't keep her *and* the kittens, so we kept a male kitten, gave the rest away, and decided to put her on her own, so we wouldn't have her giving us kittens to bother with all the time."

"What did you think was going to happen to her?"

He looked blank for a moment and then said, "Oh, you know, they always find homes. There was a trailer camp right where we dropped her off."

I asked him if he was aware that shelters have to rescue millions of abandoned pets every year because owners tell themselves someone else will take in their unwanted animals. He again looked blank. Then I had one more question for him. "What lesson do you think your children learned from what you did?"

The man looked startled, then puzzled, and then—and I give him some credit for this—he looked embarrassed. I think I got through to him. So did the $150 fine the judge imposed on him.

Many people think of a pet as property that they can dispose of at will, like a toy they have grown tired of or a houseplant that doesn't please them anymore. It never occurs to them that animals have some legal rights of their own, such as the right to certain protections from abuse.

Another thing that struck me about this case was the "magic thinking" with which the man justified what he did. Virtually all people who abandon animals convince themselves either that somebody else will come along to take care of the pet they have thrown out, or that the pet can take care of itself on its own. They tell themselves they are giving the animal its "freedom" because they don't want to admit they are abandoning it. Virtually all discarded pets get hit by cars, die of disease or injuries, starve to death, are deliberately killed by people, or are picked up and brought to animal shelters where 80 percent of them must be killed because there isn't room for all of them and nobody adopts them. So people who put a dog or cat on its own engage in fantasies and kid themselves about what they are really doing.

I don't remember when I started loving animals, or even if some particular incident made me want to help them. But I went to law school with the express purpose of becoming an advocate for animals. There is a great need for trained professionals to represent animals in our

Raining Cats and Dogs: The Treatment of Pets

courts and to enforce our anticruelty laws.

There were no courses specifically on the defense of animals at the law school I went to. The closest thing to it was environmental law, so I took that. I believe some law schools are now beginning to teach courses in animal rights. There is a growing recognition in law schools and in the courts that animals' rights should be taken seriously, but progress seems slow to me.

During summers when I was in college and law school, I worked as a legal intern for the Society for Animal Rights, a national humane organization, so I did have some background in animal protection when I graduated and came to work in my present job.

My job is prosecuting animal abuse cases like the one I just told you about. Also, I go to the state capital regularly to work on getting more animal protection laws enacted.

You would never believe the things people do to animals out of outright cruelty, neglect, or simple ignorance. I once prosecuted a woman who had raised a puppy without noticing that as the dog grew, its collar of course became tighter and tighter. She never expanded the collar. By the time we got the dog, it was in such bad shape that it had to be put to sleep.

"But I didn't know my dog was suffering," she pleaded in court.

The judge asked her the obvious question, so I didn't have to: "How could you *not* know?"

In another case I prosecuted, a man was accustomed to walking his dog long distances every day on pavement. He never noticed, he claimed, that the skin was all worn off the animal's footpads, exposing the raw flesh. It's a wonder the dog could take a single step—it must have been in agony. We took the owner to court and got him a stiff fine—and took the dog away and found a more responsible owner for it.

I prosecute more cases of neglect, such as these two, than of cruelty, such as throwing an animal out of an automobile. Apparently it is hard for some people to have empathy for their animals, so the animals badly need defending. After all, in our society ignorance and insensitivity are no excuse for neglecting a child. And neither children nor animals can defend themselves.

It is estimated that there are 52 million pet dogs and 36 million pet cats in homes in the United States today. Americans spend well over $3 billion a year on pet food. You may also have read about beauty parlors and summer camps for pets, mink coats, diamond collars—some people do buy this sort of thing for their dogs and cats. Pets now have their own psychiatrists, vitamins, T-shirts, candy, and cemeteries. Sometimes you read about a dog or cat being left a fortune in its owner's will. You might conclude from this that Americans are a nation of animal nuts who lavish all sorts of crazy indulgences on their pets.

I wish it were true. It's a fact that many people do take wonderful care of their pets, and their animals lead happy and healthy lives. But unfortunately they are the minority.

While there are about 70 million cats and dogs in homes, more than *14 million* are destroyed at shelters *every year* because no homes can be found for them. And for every animal brought to a shelter, it is estimated that there are nine starving on the streets. That's about 121 million stray cats and dogs.

Shelter workers do not put animals to sleep because they are cruel. They truly have no choice. The rate of adoptions by people who come for pets falls far below the number of animals that are brought in. Only two out of every ten animals can hope to go to homes. And often animals that are adopted are returned because the people change their minds.

People who let their cats and dogs breed so the children can see "the miracle of birth" should realize that because of the pressure of pet overpopulation, they are really causing the miracle of death!

Animal shelters everywhere get a big increase in both dogs and cats at the end of every summer. This happens particularly around summer resorts. You can probably guess the reason. People adopt a cat or dog "for the summer," and then when the time comes to go back to their homes in the cities, they feel it is too much trouble to take care of a pet, so they just leave it behind. In one beach resort I know, if you walk along the roads in September, past the boarded-up empty cottages, you'll find a starving cat or dog huddled alone on the porch of every third or fourth house.

And as laws go into effect in cities around the nation requiring people to clean up after their dogs on the street, the numbers of dogs abandoned or dropped off at shelters increase. Some people would rather get rid of their dogs than bother to clean up. The laws are basically a good idea, I think. The streets should be kept clean. But as usual, dogs wind up as victims through no fault of their own.

The domestication of dogs and cats took place many

thousands of years ago, although in the beginning they were not so much pets as working members of households. Cats lived in the barns and stables and caught the rodents; dogs were used for hunting and protection. When life was difficult and full of uncertainties for people, you better believe it was even worse for animals! It's the same today in parts of the world where there is not enough food available for the people—the animals come out a poor second in terms of who eats.

In addition, cats have had to contend for survival with the superstitions that grew up around them—that they are witches, that they are somehow associated with the devil, and other nonsense. These small animals have been subjected to the most bizarre forms of torture, which in the past was widespread and still goes on today. Even though most of the cases I prosecute in court involve animal neglect, I still come across instances of active cruelty I don't even want to remember.

Dogs and cats are caught in a bind—they are totally dependent on human beings, and yet human beings cause them the most harm. In spite of all the people who love their pets and treat them well, most people abuse them, in one way or another. The biggest killer of pet animals is accidents—and most of the accidents could be prevented if owners protected their pets. Cats fall out of windows, cats and dogs get hit by cars, they get bones stuck in their throats, dogs are left in cars that overheat in the sun—the list is endless.

A law professor I know, Henry Mark Holzer, points out that people treat their pets any way they wish because animals are regarded as property, with no more value than trivial objects. Holzer believes we should pass and implement a law whereby all pet owners would be required to have their animals tattooed with a little number, on the inside of the ear or thigh or some other visible place—a veterinarian could do it quickly and inexpensively. The number would be registered with an official agency such as the state licensing agency. Then, if an animal were found wandering, or dead, the owner could be traced. And if owners were found guilty of deliberate abandonment or negligence and fined, they might not be so quick next time to take on an animal "for the summer" or "for the children" or whatever. And if they couldn't keep it, they would more likely take it to a shelter rather than throw it out and risk having to pay a sizable fine.

Unfortunately the conditions in some animal shelters (and pounds) are nightmarish, and many still use the decompression chamber to kill the animals that aren't adopted. Dogs and cats are locked in a cylinder that is slid into a machine that decompresses the oxygen, killing the animals. Hopefully, the animals lose consciousness rapidly, but no one knows if they suffer or not. Shelters are often short on money and inadequately staffed. They are infrequently inspected because there is little public money set aside to employ inspectors to enforce the laws that apply to shelters. Unfortunately, animal welfare matters have a low priority in our legal system.

Worst of all are the so-called puppy mills that supply puppies to the pet stores. Some of these places are beyond description, with animals in cages stacked three and four on top of each other, with wire mesh floors that allow the wastes of the animals to run through—often onto the animals in cages below them. The wire mesh floors in the cages also cause the puppies' legs and feet to grow weak, and sometimes a puppy's paw will get caught and hurt on the wire.

The females in puppy mills are not allowed to rest between litters, and some of them are so weakened from continual birthing that they can hardly stand. Most of the puppies are worm-infested and sickly by the time they are delivered to the pet shops, but the shops accept them and sell them anyway.

The Department of Agriculture is supposed to inspect puppy mills, and occasionally they do close down a really bad one. But like everything else involving animals, there aren't enough inspectors, or enough diligent inspectors, to seriously threaten the business, so the puppy mills prosper.

In our state, our agency can use the anticruelty laws to prosecute the owners of puppy mills with animals that are suffering. We routinely inspect pet stores, and I have prosecuted several shop owners for having sick animals, or unsanitary or overcrowded conditions. In one pet store, one of our inspectors found a dead puppy.

"I thought he was asleep," this shopkeeper said when I questioned him in court.

But we don't just prosecute and fine the shop owners; we also remove the animals when conditions are bad. Of course, that just increases the overload of pets in our shelter. I personally think people should stop buying dogs and cats from pet shops or breeders until the millions that are in shelters are placed in homes. Many people think that if they pay money—often several hundred dollars—for a pedigreed animal, they are getting a superior one. But what does "superior" mean? More beautiful? More healthy? More intelligent or loving?

Raining Cats and Dogs: The Treatment of Pets

Nobody can claim pet-store animals are superior to shelter animals in these respects—and shelter animals are a lot less expensive.

Some people do enjoy the specific characteristics of certain breeds, and insist they get more pleasure from animals with these particular traits—the lovely color of a blue point Siamese cat, for example, or the beautiful head of a collie. The pedigreed pets at our shelter are nearly always adopted quickly. But it's a curious situation that on the one hand breeders and owners of pedigreed animals are bringing more and more salable puppies and kittens into the world, while at the same time the shelters are putting more and more puppies and kittens to death because homes cannot be found for them. Isn't that a paradox?

There is another angle to this strange situation. Animal shelters are supported by taxes or public donations. It costs a great deal of money to round up and capture strays, accept strays or pets brought in by the public, and care for these unwanted animals. It's expensive to feed and shelter them and then destroy those for whom homes can't be found. So ordinary taxpayers, as well as people who donate money to shelters, have to support unthinking pet owners who dump their dogs and cats or allow their pets to bring more animals into the world.

"I wish I could live in the country, where Fiorello could get out and have a good sex life," said a city-dwelling friend of mine about her handsome black male kitten.

My friend doesn't realize what she is saying. She would allow her cat to father kittens—who, of course, would not be her problem but the problem of the owners of the many female cats with whom Fiorello would have "a good sex life." Most of these owners would have to destroy the kittens, abandon them, or bring them to shelters—which the rest of us would then have to pay for. Leaving aside the humane considerations, I'm surprised the dollars-and-cents problem of pet overpopulation hasn't made taxpayers demand more low-cost spay and neuter clinics.

Some people still think they are depriving their pets of something terribly important to the pet by having it neutered. They confuse their pets' sexuality with their own, but actually the animal never knows it is missing anything at all. Also, neutering will not change an animal's temperament or make it lazy or fat. The only thing that will make a pet fat is being overfed by its owner—unless the pet learns to open the refrigerator!

Spay and neutering operations are performed by a veterinarian. Neutering means a simple castration (removal of testes) for a male; it is inexpensive and over in a minute. A spay operation (removal of the uterus and ovaries) for a female is less simple but still not serious. It costs a little more and requires a day or two at the vet's or in the animal hospital. Many cities now have clinics where people can get low-cost spaying and neutering operations for their pets. Maybe in the future the situation with stray dogs and cats will get so bad that these operations will be required by law—and perhaps we need such a law. It would certainly be cheaper for the public to support clinics where people could have their pets neutered for little or no money than to spend what it costs to round up, keep, and destroy homeless ones.

The other day as I was leaving my office I saw a dog that had just been turned over to our shelter. The owner

Raining Cats and Dogs: The Treatment of Pets

was walking out of the building, and the dog was being led away by one of our shelter workers. The dog seemed completely bewildered and kept looking over its shoulder at its owner's retreating back; it tried to break away and run after him. As the door closed I heard the dog begin to howl pitifully.

I couldn't help wondering—how did this happen? Had the owner really wanted to keep his animal and couldn't? Or had he decided it was just too much trouble? The dog, of course, had no control over what was happening to it. Even a young, healthy animal can be condemned to death if its owner gets tired of it—and death is usually better than abandonment.

Sometimes people ask me if I run into any problems being taken seriously as a lawyer because I am young and a woman. I don't think so. One of my friends, another lawyer, thinks it may be an asset, especially since I am rather soft-spoken and I don't seem very aggressive. I always try to control my anger when I'm prosecuting an animal abuse case. In my experience, I have found that I can appeal to judges better that way, and also perhaps make people feel guilty about harming their pets, so they won't do it again.

The writer Paul Gallico, a cat lover, once wrote to his pet cat, who was purring on his lap one evening: "Do not be too proud or smug, for somewhere your counterpart is dragging itself through wretched days and nights into oblivion because luck has passed it by, and for those hidden in the darkness beyond the lights of our windows there is no justice."

Well, people like me are trying our best to get a little justice for those other cats hiding in the darkness.

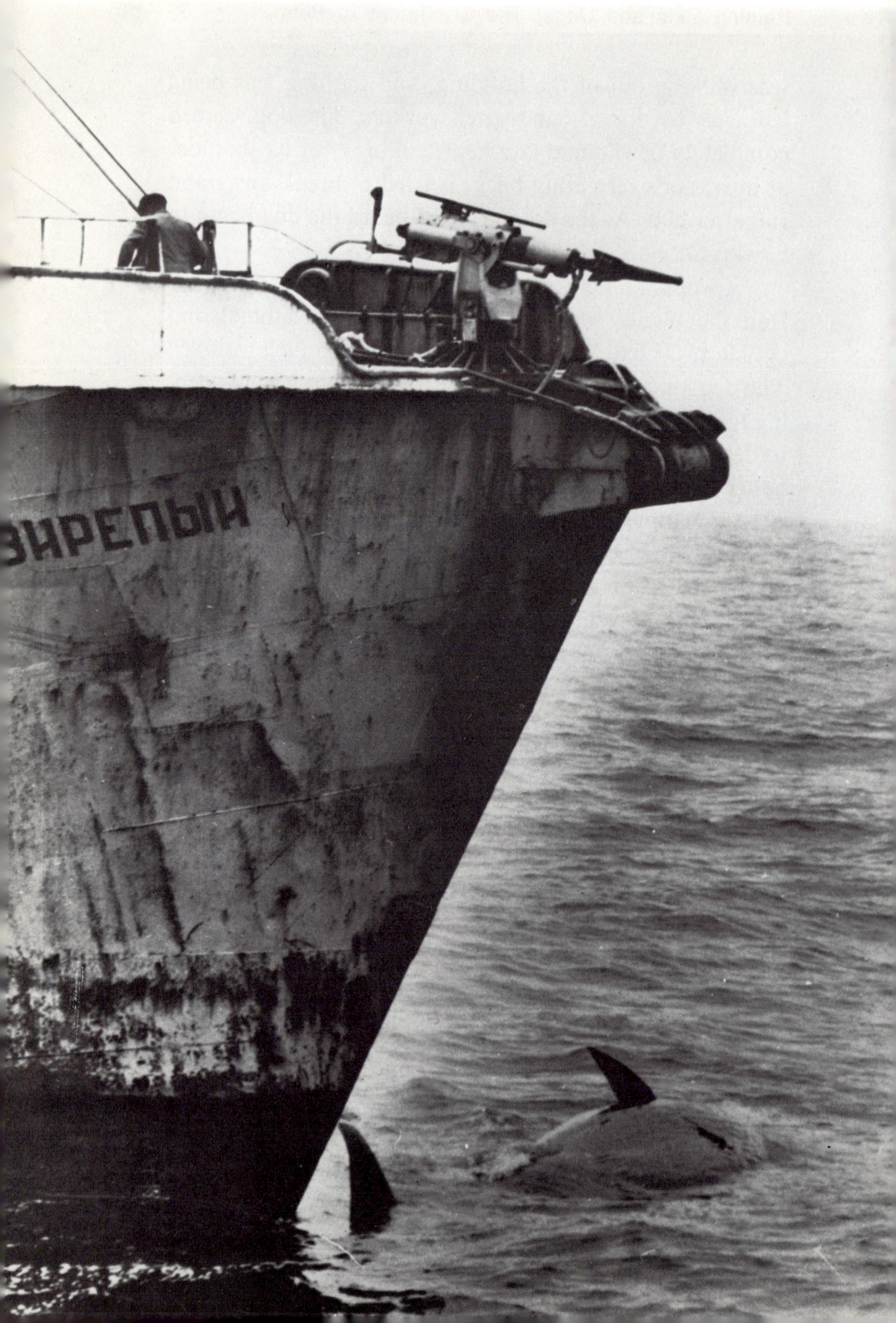

3

PEACEABLE GIANTS:
The Extinction of Whales

*Colin Jones and Pete Meltzer
are two young men
who love whales.*

It was our second day in the Gulf of Honduras just south of Mexico. My buddy Pete and I were skimming along in the seventeen-foot canoe we had sailed and paddled all the way from Connecticut. We had been gone nearly six months on our expedition to bring the message of saving the whales to as many people as possible. We had met and talked to maybe a couple of thousand people and had some encounters with dolphins, but had seen only a few whales way in the distance as we rounded the Yucatán Peninsula in the Gulf of Mexico. Caution for our own safety kept us from venturing more than a mile and a half from shore. It would have been foolishly dangerous to go out farther, much as we wanted to see more whales.

Now it was late afternoon and we were hugging the coast looking for a little village where we might dock our boat, talk to some people about whales, and spend the night. The sun's rays were slanting over the mountains in the distance, west of us. There was a nice breeze, the water was calm, and we were slipping along silently, keeping our eyes on the nearby shore. Pete was sitting back of me in the canoe, holding the tiller. Suddenly I heard him gasp.

"We've got company." His voice wasn't loud, but he sure sounded excited. I looked around.

A huge shape was gliding through the water parallel to us, only about twenty-five feet away. About ten feet of its back was above the surface, but the entire creature was more than twice as long as our boat.

Excitement rose in me with such a rush I almost couldn't breathe. Let me tell you, a whale is one awesome sight. And yet, I felt no fear whatsoever.

Pete and I just sat there in our boat, not moving, frozen with fascination. The animal's back was dark, really black, and we got a glimpse of a long flipper. We recognized it as a humpback whale. Humpbacks winter in tropical waters.

The whale hung in the water beside us for a short while. It seemed to be looking us over. Then, as quietly as it had appeared, it sank below the surface, turned away from us, and slowly disappeared. We were speechless for several seconds.

"Wow!" breathed Pete, reaching for the binoculars.

"Remember what that fellow from the cetacean society said to us last year, before we left Connecticut?" I asked him, referring to an organization that works to protect cetaceans—whales, dolphins, and porpoises.

Peaceable Giants: The Extinction of Whales

"I was just thinking the same thing," he replied.

When we were making our plans for this trip, we had many conferences with everyone we could find who knew anything about whales. At the end of a long conversation with one very knowledgeable man, he had given us an odd look.

"You'll probably think I'm crazy, but I'm going to tell you something," he said. "When you start on this mission of yours to save the whales, you won't believe it now, but *they'll know you're coming.*"

The best part of this experience in the Gulf of Honduras was yet to come, and I'll tell you about it later. But first let me explain to you how I happened to be sailing a canoe in this part of the world in the first place. When I was a kid, we spent many summer vacations on Long Island in Sag Harbor, a town that had once been a busy whaling village. I used to visit the whaling museum. There were many relics from the whaling ships displayed there, and pictures of whaling scenes, but it wasn't so much the lore of the whale hunts that interested me. I was fascinated by the creatures themselves. My parents gave me books about whales, and our school library had some, too. I liked to read about these sea animals.

Whales, as you probably know, are not fish but mammals that breathe air and give birth to young that are called calves. In fact, when a female whale gives birth, she immediately lifts her infant to the surface on her back so it can breathe, and keeps raising it until it is able to swim to the surface for itself. Typically, another female whale stays nearby during the birth and keeps watch for danger and will defend the infant along with the mother if necessary. Mother whales nurse their infants just as cows and horses do. They are devotedly protective and have been known to die trying to save their calves from whalers. Whales live in family groups called pods and often show concern and consideration for each other—especially those that are mates. There are known instances of whales risking danger to stay with mates in trouble.

Whales have thick blankets of fat covering their bodies to keep them warm in the ocean depths and in the coldest arctic waters where many types of whales prefer to live. The littlest whale, the pygmy sperm, is only about thirteen feet long, but the blue whale, the largest creature that has ever lived on our planet, grows to as long as a hundred feet. The blue has been hunted so close to extinction that it might not exist as a species for many more years. In fact, at least half of the ten species of the so-called great whales may already be done for.

Most whales eat krill, which are shrimplike crustaceans found just below the water's surface, although some whales dive to tremendous depths—several thousand feet—to capture giant squid. The whale gets its locomotion from its enormous tail, which is roughly equal to a 500-horsepower engine. Jacques Cousteau, the famous underwater explorer, writer, and filmmaker, says that a diver who brushes against one of the larger whales has the impression of having just had an encounter with a speeding locomotive.

We are just beginning to learn about these fabulous animals. We know that they have huge, complex brains, larger and in some ways more developed than the brains of human beings. We are only beginning to discover the depth and breadth of their intelligence. They have a sophisticated communications system, and their "songs" are transmitted underwater for hundreds of miles.

What has perhaps fascinated people most of all about these giant animals is their gentleness. There is no documented instance of an unprovoked whale attacking a human being. Long ago when whales were hunted with simple harpoons in small boats, a wounded whale could turn on its tormentors with deadly effect. But divers who have swum among whales swear that the animals are not only friendly and harmless but are aware of how weak human beings are compared to themselves. They seem to know that one accidental stroke of their tails or fins, one bump, could kill a person. Cousteau says that in some of the underwater films his crew has made, you can see humpback whales lift their flippers carefully to avoid hitting divers as they glide past them.

I could go on and on about these marvelous animals. I never lost my interest in them, even while I was growing up and going to architecture school. For the past few years I've mostly been designing vacation homes—small, simple, solar-energy houses or modern underground houses in the woods, mountains, and at the shore. I haven't made a lot of money, but I love my work. My favorite project so far was designing a veterinary hospital. The group of veterinarians for whom I did the job were willing to spend enough to make it really well equipped and especially humane and comfortable for the animals.

Still, at times I've been restless, and when I got the idea for this trip, I decided to take it before I became more involved in work or had a family, when it would be hard to get away. The times in your life when you can drop what you're doing for a year or two to have an adventure like the one Pete and I were having just don't come along every day.

Pete and I were sitting around my living room one day, having a beer and watching a TV documentary on whales. Pete is a skilled carpenter, a real craftsman. We got to know each other through work. He had built some of my houses. Now he had just returned from a job in another part of Connecticut, and I had just finished a house in Vermont. We hadn't seen each other for several months.

The TV documentary was really interesting—full of information about different kinds of whales and their habits and behavior. At the end, a whale hunt was shown, with the huge, swift whaling ships using sonar and even a helicopter to locate the fleeing animals. Some whales can stay underwater for long periods, but eventually they have to come to the surface for air. Finally a big one had to surface, and the helicopter spotted him. The whaler launched a two-hundred-pound iron harpoon from a cannon. The harpoon had a grenade attached that was timed to go off seconds after the harpoon entered the animal's body. The grenade blew up inside the whale, but the animal lived for hours in agony, as they sometimes do. Its blood stained the sea for miles. Finally, it was hauled to the factory ship, hoisted aboard, and soon was turned into industrial oil, fertilizer, animal food, and products for perfume, soap, detergent, shampoo, varnish, and gelatin.

The TV documentary was very effective. It had

Peaceable Giants: The Extinction of Whales

shown these beautiful, rare, harmless animals performing their underwater ballets and swimming in friendly curiosity around the underwater photographers. We had heard their calls and songs and even seen some unusual sequences of whales playing with each other and courting. Then we had seen the chase, the suffering, and the bloody death. Pete and I sat there for a little while, in silence. Both of us were moved.

"Did you know that one of these animals is killed every thirty minutes?" I asked Pete. "About twenty-four thousand are wiped out every year."

"And there's almost nothing we can do as individuals to stop it," replied Pete gloomily. "I've signed petitions, boycotted goods from the big whaling nations, sent letters, the works. But nothing seems to make a dent."

Pete was right. In spite of years of protest by millions of people the world over, Japan and the Soviet Union continue to whale and are responsible for 85 percent of the killing. Iceland, Denmark, Norway, Spain, Cyprus, Peru, Chile, and South Korea—the nations that do most of the rest—also are still at it.

Way back in 1946, the countries that did a lot of whaling began to realize that if they kept killing whales at the rate they were doing it, they would soon eliminate all the whales on earth. So they formed the International Whaling Commission to get together every year, review the situation of each whale species, and agree on the numbers of those species that could be killed in the coming year. The object of the commission is to save the whaling industries of the world, not to save the whales for their own sakes.

The United States has led the fight within the Whaling Commission to put limits on the killing. But when the United Nations Committee on the Environment recommended that everybody stop killing whales for ten years, to prevent the most threatened species from becoming extinct, the International Whaling Commission refused to agree to even a limited moratorium. In 1979, the Whaling Commission belatedly declared a one-year moratorium on all factory-ship whaling. It remains to be seen if this moratorium will be honored by the Japanese and the Russians. Whatever happens, it may be too late to save some species.

Groups of people all over the world concerned with the plight of the whales have formed protection organizations such as Greenpeace and Project Jonah. Also, national humane and environmental organizations such as the Fund for Animals, Friends of the Earth, Animal Welfare Institute, and the Cousteau Society have pressed for help for the whales.

For several days after Pete and I had seen the film on whales, I kept being nudged by this little thought in the back of my mind. Everybody who is interested in whales is aware of how little the average person actually knows about them. Most people have never had the opportunity to see a real whale and probably never will. It occurred to me that if more people knew what these animals are really like, they might care whether or not they were hunted to extinction.

I realized my own knowledge of them was limited compared to the real experts. But on the other hand, I thought, suppose I simply went and told what I know to

Peaceable Giants: The Extinction of Whales

as many people as I could get to listen to me, and got them to sign petitions to save the whales. I might not change history—but then again, I might. At least I would feel I was doing my part, I would be putting my beliefs on the line. I was at a point in my life where I could do such a thing.

If I went driving across the country, I would use up gasoline and spend a lot of money for what might be a limited success. It would be hard to get people in Kansas, for example, turned on to whales. Talking to people in cities and towns along both coasts of the United States made more sense. And because of my childhood summers at Sag Harbor, I knew how to handle small boats.

Well, to make a long story short, I decided to make the trip by water—down the east coast of the United States, Mexico, and Central America, through the Panama Canal, up the west coast of the continent as far as Vancouver, Canada. To make the trip less dangerous and lonely, I asked Pete to join me, and after giving it some thought, he agreed. A boat company gave us our heavy, almost unsinkable fiber glass canoe. Other people gave us equipment. We both brushed up on our Spanish. We interested a cetacean society in helping us organize and publicize our mission. Then we took all our savings, which didn't add up to much but made enough to start with, and one bright fall day we were off.

So far, we had met with all sorts of adventures, mostly good. Every night we had landed in some town or city, except for a few times in unpopulated areas when we had just pulled our canoe ashore and slept in our pup tent on the beach. I think we really succeeded in mobilizing some public opinion for saving the whales. We had collected thousands of signatures. I know we reached a lot of people who might not have thought about the whales one way or the other if we hadn't come along.

We also included the dolphins and porpoises in our message. Some scientists consider dolphins and porpoises the same family. These playful, graceful, friendly animals are rarely hunted as whales are, but they are often killed by accident. Vast numbers of them have been a casualty of the tuna-fishing industry. Because dolphins often congregate around schools of tuna, the tuna boats rely on the dolphins to help them locate the tuna. Then they cast their huge nets, accidentally capturing dophins along with the tuna—the dolphins become entangled in the tuna nets and drown. Fortunately, the pressure from public opinion and boycotts has finally forced the tuna-fishing companies to use a different method of fishing that allows many of the dolphins to get out of the net before they drown.

In 1978 a bunch of Japanese fishermen drove a school of hundreds of dolphins ashore and clubbed them to death because they said the dolphins were eating the fish they wanted to catch. They called the dolphins "predators," a word that has an evil sound, though it simply means any animal whose natural diet is other animals rather than plants. Dolphins can hardly be blamed for seeking their natural diet of small fish, can they? People the world over were outraged at the fishermen's attack on the dolphins.

One day we were sailing along off the east coast of Florida, near Cape Kennedy, when suddenly we heard a splash just behind us. We both turned, and there was a

Peaceable Giants: The Extinction of Whales

dolphin with its head out of water, sort of grinning at us.

"Hi, fella," I said. The animal dived gracefully underwater and disappeared with a flick of its tail. But about thirty seconds later, it popped up on the other side of our canoe and looked at us again.

It was obvious it was curious and had just swum up for a good look at us. It reappeared several times. When it realized we were friendly, it began to play with us. It never came too close, but seemed to think it was fun to surprise us by appearing in a different place time after time. We began to laugh and applaud every time the dolphin made one of its wonderful arched leaps out of the water.

Our new friend stayed with us for about an hour, and then we entered a cove where we saw a dock we could tie up at. It was late in the day, we had come a good distance and were tired, so we headed in. Sure enough, the dolphin swam along with us. We didn't think anything much about it, because we knew he'd go back out to sea when he saw we were landing.

But as we approached the dock, something ugly happened. A couple of men came running down the dock with guns in their hands. For a few seconds, we thought they were going to shoot at us! But then, we saw they were shouting and pointing at the water behind us. They were going to shoot the dolphin! We yelled at them to stop. They began to shoot. They emptied their guns at the water where the dolphin had disappeared.

We were thunderstruck. These two guys had come out to kill a dolphin just for the fun of it!

Then the men looked at us and our canoe. We were

both deeply suntanned and had beards. Our clothes were pretty worn out. They stared at our sail, with a picture of a whale and the inscription "Save the Whale" on it.

"Y'all going to save the whale in that little ole boat?" one of the men said, and they began to laugh.

Pete and I looked at each other and decided, without having to say a word, that if these guys represented the folks around this part of Florida, we didn't feel like talking about whales tonight. We changed our course and headed back out of the cove, and continued to sail for another hour till we found another place to stop. We had encountered heckling before, and every now and then someone had thought we were crazy and told us so. True, our mission was to persuade people, and to try to change their thinking, but this incident had sickened us.

There have been so many stories, down through history since earliest times, of sailors who have been shipwrecked or fallen overboard and have been saved by dolphins. The stories say that when the sailors were struggling in the water, dolphins appeared and buoyed them up with their bodies and pushed them to shore. In more modern times, people used to think those stories were just fairy tales. But now as we learn more about these smart, congenial animals, the stories seem very likely to be true. It is known, for example, that mother dolphins lift their newborn calves to the surface to breathe, just as mother whales do. And scientists who study dolphins are continually reporting acts of kindness that these animals extend to one another—including instances of dolphins lifting injured dolphins to the surface and aiding them in other amazing ways. It is not at all improbable that they would behave that way toward helpless people in the water.

The major danger to the dolphins of the world, and eventually to all marine animals, is pollution. Jacques Cousteau believes our waters are very sick. The organization he founded, the Cousteau Society, is exploring ways to keep our oceans from becoming so polluted that no life can exist in them. It sounds impossible, doesn't it, because the oceans are so vast, but he and many other scientists who study the sea are trying to call our attention to the very real danger before it is too late.

Pete and I hope to meet up with the Greenpeace people and perhaps be allowed to join one of their expeditions to interfere with actual whale hunts. Greenpeace is a Canadian-based organization of environmentalists with chapters in many countries. Every year during the whale-hunting season, Greenpeace members in ships search the oceans looking for whalers. When they find a hunt going on with the whalers chasing and closing in on some whales, the Greenpeace volunteers jump into small rubber powerboats launched from their ships, and harass the whalers by getting between the hunters and the whales. Often this interference has enabled some whales to escape. So far, none of the whaling ships has harpooned the little rubber boats, though they have come close to running over them, and harpoons have whizzed by just over the Greenpeace people's heads. The Greenpeace activists are not much more than a nuisance to the Russian, Japanese, and Icelandic whaling industries, but they certainly call attention to the ruthlessness and brutality of whale hunting.

That is what Pete and I, in our far less spectacular

way, were trying to do, of course. And we especially tried to carry the message that there are available substitutes for all whale products. Very few people need whale meat to eat, for instance, and few whales are considered edible. Some Japanese and Eskimos eat whales, but since the Japanese export so much fish, and fish is a first-rate source of protein, it can hardly be said that the Japanese people would suffer from protein deprivation if they didn't get whale meat.

As for the fine oil that whales provide, there is a little desert plant called the jojoba whose seeds yield an oil that is just as good as whale oil. The jojoba plant grows easily and could be cultivated indefinitely.

If enough people worldwide boycotted products containing whale substances and instead pressured for the development and use of substitutes, the end of whaling would be possible.

It is a source of mystery to me why whales, who for thousands of years have suffered little but pain and death at the hands of human beings, are still so benevolent toward us. Whales do not interfere with people in any way; they do not attack us when we venture into their element, the sea. Also, they use nothing that we ourselves need. They are one of the earth's great marvels and deserve to live. We owe it to them, and to future generations of human beings, to allow them to continue.

Getting back to the humpback whale that checked us out in the Gulf of Honduras. We saw its vapory, almost balloon-shaped spout a few times after it dived and left us, and then we turned our attention back to the shore. A little while passed.

Suddenly we saw the whale's spout again quite near us, and not far from that, one of these immense creatures leaped from the water in a great arch, landing with a thundering splash. Its entire forty-foot body seemed oddly graceful, not at all clumsy. As Pete and I were gaping at that, another whale leaped, and then another. The water seemed to explode with whales, spouting and leaping and rolling. It was a fireworks of whales! We couldn't always tell whether we were seeing two whales leap successively, one after the other, or one whale making two successive leaps—but we are sure there must have been five or six of them.

Maybe we just happened to catch a number of whales at sport, having a good time among themselves. But Pete and I both hoped that the show was for us—maybe it was a celebration of our mission.

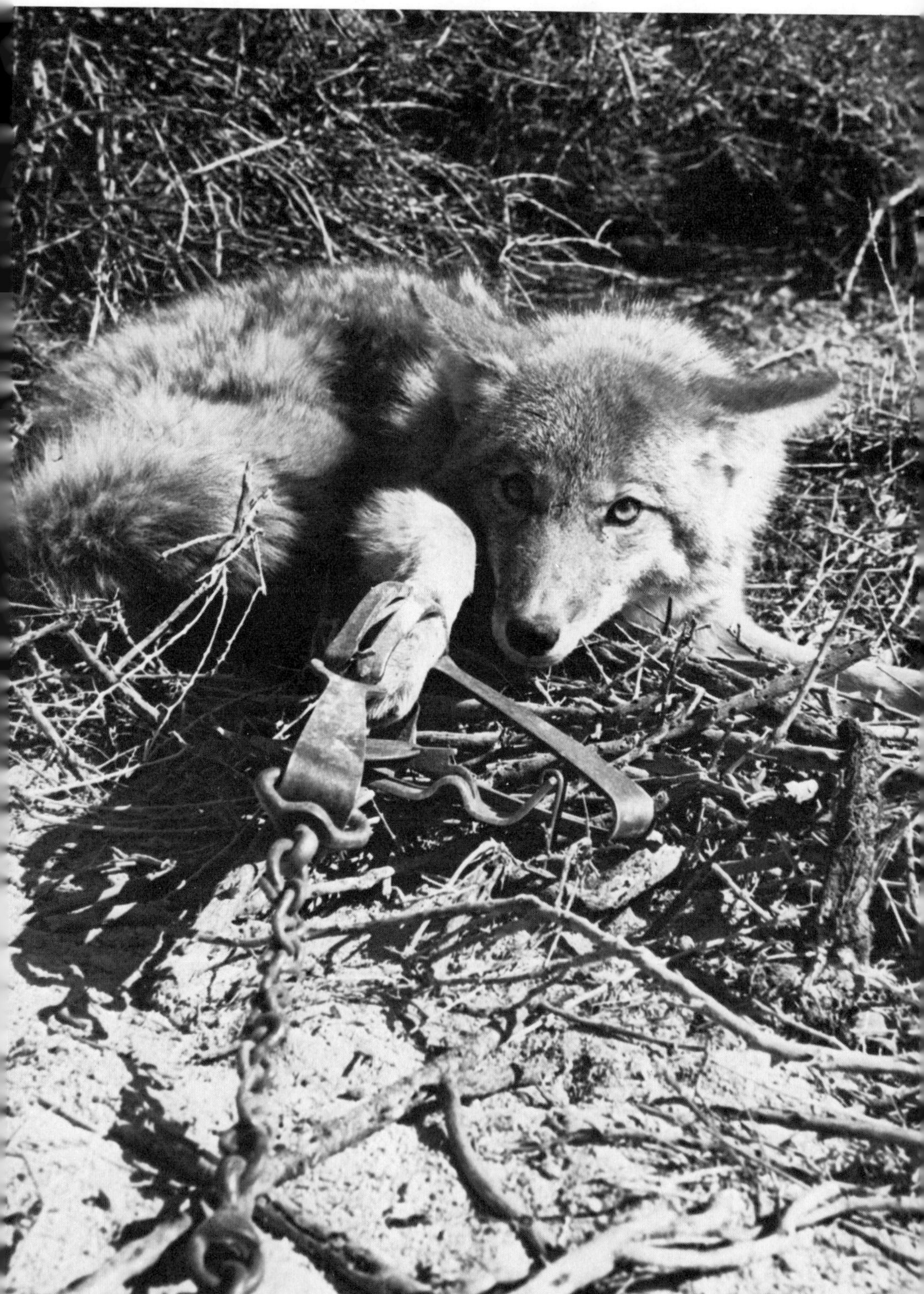

4

WHOSE WILDLIFE?
Hunting and Trapping

Nora Clausen is an illustrator who specializes in wildlife.

ONE morning in early winter as I was cleaning up the kitchen after breakfast, I heard the guns again and they sounded awfully close. Our land, up here in the woods just below the Canadian border, is posted against hunting, but hunters sometimes ignore our signs and come into the woods anyhow. This alarms us very much because not only do we have many pets that might be walking in the woods, but also our acres are full of wildlife. We detest sport hunting, and the animals on our land are protected. Our property is a private sanctuary for all wild creatures.

Joe, my husband, had taken the pickup truck and gone into the village on an errand, so I was alone in the house. I went and got our .22, loaded it, and went out onto our patio facing the woods. I aimed the gun at the sky and fired five or six shots. I really made a lot of noise.

When I finished firing, I went in the house and stood just inside the door, listening, for quite a while, but I didn't hear another shot from the hunters.

"Good!" I thought to myself. "I scared those bums away." I went back to stacking the dishwasher, humming to myself. Suddenly Lars, our big dog (part golden retriever, part who knows?) came bounding across our yard, panting. He seemed very excited. He peered through the heavy glass kitchen door and wagged his tail hard.

"What is it, Lars?" I asked, opening the door. The dog wheeled and dashed across the frozen lawn, then stopped and looked back at me.

"Lars!" I called. "Who do you think you are—Lassie?" He had never done this before. Lars is a wonderfully good-natured dog; he gets along with other animals and virtually all people. We have sometimes wondered if he had any skills as a watchdog, but then he has never been required to do any guarding. We love him for his personality. Apparently, we had underestimated his intelligence. It was clear he wanted me to follow him now. Was it possible there was someone or something in the woods that my dog thought I should see? "All right, Lars, I'm coming," I called.

I pulled on a coat and set off, with Lars running ahead of me. Every now and then he would stop and wait for me to catch up. He led me a good distance—about a mile into the thick forest.

Suddenly he stopped and stood, wagging his tail and

Whose Wildlife? Hunting and Trapping

gazing at something. I approached very quietly. By this time I figured I would find an animal those hunters had killed or wounded and left behind when they heard my warning shots.

It was an animal all right—a magnificent red fox. It wasn't dead or wounded from the hunters' bullets. The fox was caught in a trap—one of those leg-hold traps that doesn't kill the animal but holds it tightly by one leg.

The poor animal looked at me in total despair. It was half-frozen, and too weak and frightened to struggle; it must have been there a long time, maybe a couple of days. I knew enough not to try to free it myself—wild animals fear human beings above anything else, and in its fright and pain this fox might bite me.

I must have run all the way back to our house. I called our good friend Alvin Campbell, a veterinarian, who lives not far away and takes care of all our pets and, on many occasions, sick or injured wild animals that we shelter.

"Alvin, this is Nora," I said. "Somebody set a leg-hold trap in our woods and caught a fox. Lars found it. I don't know how long it has been there, but it looks in bad shape. Can you come?" Alvin, bless him, said he'd be right over.

I was worried that the trapper would return in the meantime and kill the fox, pick up the trap, and escape. But the trapped animal was still there, panting in its agony. Alvin had brought along a few medical tools and wore heavy gloves. He managed to inject the fox with a tranquilizer while I distracted it with a bowl of water from a small thermos I had brought. When we backed away and waited for the drug to take effect, it lapped a little water.

Finally we could see the fox was in less pain, thoroughly relaxed and half-asleep, so we freed him from the trap. Alvin wrapped him in his jacket and carried him. I unchained the trap and brought it back to the house with us. I noticed there was no owner's name or number engraved on it, though legally there should have been.

Alvin took the animal into our barn and examined his paw carefully. The leg above where the trap had held it was grotesquely swollen and bruised and had some terrible cuts where the fox himself had probably chewed it. Animals sometimes bite themselves trying to get at what is hurting them. Alvin didn't think the paw was broken, however. He gave the animal an injection of antibiotics and something to reduce the swelling of the leg.

I made a nest for the fox in one of the box stalls at the back of the barn, and Alvin placed him gently on a pile of hay. I decided against putting a blanket or towels there for him to lie on because they would have our human smell on them. The fox was going to be frightened enough when he came to and found himself confined in the stall—why add to his distress? I left the bowl of water near him and put out food for him to eat when he woke up.

Joe came home just after Alvin left, and we tiptoed out to the barn to have a look at the unconscious fox.

"That's a handsome specimen," whispered Joe. "Is it a male or female?"

"Male," I said. As we walked back to the house, we

decided that by this time of the year he wouldn't have a female and some kits who were depending on him for food. After foxes mate, early in the year, the male stays with the female until she gives birth in the spring, and then he carries food to her the entire time she is nursing her young. The male fox works hard to feed the mother as well as himself. He brings in mice, rats, rabbits, ground-nesting birds, eggs, sometimes fruits and berries, and, if he can get them, chickens. Farmers hate foxes because they are such clever barnyard thieves. The animals take chances and raid barnyards mostly when they're hunting for more than just themselves.

When I showed Joe the trap, he said some uncomplimentary things about the person who had come onto our land and set it. We know all our neighbors and everybody in our village, and couldn't think of anyone who would set a trap on our property. Some of our neighbors do hunt and trap, but they don't do it on posted land—property lines are usually respected around here. But, of course, somebody could easily have come from any other community for miles around.

"How do we know that's the only trap in our woods?" I asked.

"We don't. I think I'll go and have a look around for any clues where you found this one." Joe and Lars set off, following the tracks Alvin, Lars, and I had made in the thin snow.

When land is posted, it means anybody caught even trespassing on it can be arrested—and the penalty is greater for someone hunting or trapping on it. And if a cow is shot or a pet trapped, the fine is really stiff. Also, there are fines for trapping without a license—although where we live youngsters under eighteen, who do most of the trapping, are not required to have licenses.

Joe and I moved to this remote part of the country seven years ago. We have several hundred acres, mostly woodland. Our property abounds in wildlife—raccoons, squirrels, porcupines, weasels, rabbits, skunks, woodchucks, opossums, beavers, muskrats. We have seen a few lynxes and bobcats, and occasionally, deer.

The reason we have so many wild animals concentrated on our property is not just because the hunting and trapping in other parts of this country drives them our way; the main reason is the problem faced by wild animals all over the world: loss of habitat. With the spread of cities and towns and the takeover of land by people for agriculture, industries, and recreation, wild animals are caught in a squeeze. They are driven from one area to another as their living space disappears.

Joe writes books and magazine articles about wildlife and I illustrate them—that's what we do for a living. Our work has been pretty successful and enables us to maintain this place and all our animals. Besides Lars, our pets include Hansel the dachshund, seven cats, Heidi our nanny goat, and Bravo and Lady, the saddle horses. Maintaining our wildlife refuge and sheltering the injured creatures that convalesce with us is one of our favorite projects. Obviously, the reason Lars knew to fetch me when he found the fox was that for years he has seen us taking care of wild animals. One spring, we found ourselves nursing seventy-seven different injured animals and birds. Some we had found, others were brought to us by people who heard we take care of injured wild animals, and Alvin had treated them all. We only have them with us temporarily—as soon as an animal recovers, we always release it.

Except for a few who have never left. Homer the woodchuck has been with us for nearly four years. He doesn't come in the house, though he hibernates every winter in a burrow under the barn. We don't consider him a pet in the true sense of the word, but he is quite tame and loves the apples and carrots we feed him. One raccoon comes back every spring with a new mate. All summer the couple and their offspring hang around our place and show up for dinner. They walk right into the kitchen, if we let them.

Joe and I make a point of accepting invitations to give talks and slide shows on wildlife to schoolchildren and other groups. We've discovered that some folks simply never think of wild animals as creatures with a value other than their fur or meat. We soften our statements against hunting when we speak at schools in rural parts of the state, because many of the kids have parents or older brothers and sisters who hunt or trap. We simply tell the kids what we know about wild animals and birds and try to nourish their interest and sensitivity to the suffering of wild animals who are hunted and trapped; we also stress the animals' role in the ecosystem and the advantage that will come to all of us if wild animals are allowed to flourish. We find the young people we talk to are very receptive; they want to learn about wild animals and enjoy watching them. Some of them, however, think of hunting and trapping as participating in nature.

Nobody knows how many people in the United States are trappers. A good guess by the Department of Commerce is about 2 million; they kill an estimated 12 million animals each year in traps. Most trappers are young people under eighteen.

Every state has laws that direct how often trappers must visit their traps—every twenty-four or forty-eight hours, or in some places, once a week. Whatever the requirement, there is no way in the world to enforce such laws. How is a game warden to supervise every man, woman, and child who traps? How can the warden know when they set their traps and how many days go by before they visit them? The laws are really useless, and dying animals endure many hours and days of torture in traps.

Some humane groups think the only hope for making trapping less cruel is to get more humane traps into widespread use. The leg-hold trap is considered so cruel that some states (and many countries) have banned it. The big problem with the leg-hold trap is that it does just what its name implies—catches and holds an animal by the leg. The animal dies a slow death, suffering from pain, cold, hunger, thirst, loss of blood, shock, or it may be killed by another animal. Imagine a rabbit caught in a leg-hold trap if a hungry bobcat happens by. Those animals that do survive until the trapper gets there are finally bludgeoned to death.

Many, many animals have been known to chew off their legs in their efforts to free themselves. Nursing mothers especially are likely to do this in order to return to their young. Joe and I often see wild animals that are missing one or two legs. Traps for beavers are set underwater and kill the animals they catch by drowning, but considerable numbers of beavers must get caught in leghold traps on land, because we see quite a few three-legged and even two-legged beavers.

Many humanitarians regard the Conibear trap as more humane than the leg-hold. Named after its inventor, a trapper himself, it is designed to kill instantly by breaking the animal's neck or backbone. But even its inventor admitted that the trap does not always kill instantly because it obviously can't be selective. If a small type of Conibear happens to catch a large animal, or vice versa, the animal will suffer intensely because the trap will catch it in some part of the body other than the neck. Also, the Conibear trap is more expensive and more complicated to set than the leghold, and a person can get badly hurt by one. For these reasons the Conibear is rejected by most trappers, particularly children.

One tragic side effect of trapping is that as many as two-thirds of the animals caught are nontarget animals—creatures not wanted for their pelts but who wander into the traps by mistake. And as residential areas grow, the numbers of pet dogs and cats that get trapped are increasing.

One of our neighbors lost a beloved pet, a sturdy German shepherd, in a Conibear trap. The poor animal pulled the trap from its stake and dragged herself three hundred feet to home, where her owner found her collapsed in the driveway. He couldn't even pry the trap apart without help, and rushed her to Alvin. But her windpipe was crushed, vertebrae cracked, arteries and veins burst, and she died in excruciating pain.

Joe and I have examined many traps, and the cage trap is the most humane we know of, comparatively speaking, because it doesn't crush the animal. But cage traps are more expensive and heavier to carry to location. Maybe a farmer trying to catch a fox who is eating his chickens or a woodchuck who is destroying his vegetable garden might use a cage trap, but a trapper will set a whole line of traps in the woods and isn't going to bother with the relatively cumbersome cage traps. A few humane organizations and even some members of the fur industry, under pressure from the humane groups, are trying to encourage research for the development of a truly humane trap.

Every year some sympathetic legislators in Washington introduce bills to ban leg-hold traps throughout the United States, but they are always defeated by the organized trapping groups and the fur industry. In spite of strong efforts by such groups as the Humane Society of the United States, the Society for Animal Rights, Fund for Animals, Beauty Without Cruelty, and the Friends of Animals, these proposed laws never get anywhere.

I wish we could grow away from the practice of wearing furs. I would like to see people come to believe that it is immoral and unnecessary to cause millions of animals to suffer greatly to produce clothing we don't need. It's interesting to note that our soldiers stationed in the Arctic, and even many Eskimos, don't wear furs—they wear synthetic-filled parkas. True, many furs are very beautiful. Even so, most of us would be repelled at the idea of filling our homes with stuffed real animals. How come we think it's just fine to wear parts of animals on our backs?

It's hard to rank types of trapping and hunting according to cruelty, but surely the baby-seal hunts in northern Canada have to be the most brutal. Here there isn't even the pretense of sport, for the young animals make no effort to get away and couldn't if they tried, so the sealers just walk up to them and bludgeon them to death. In the spring of 1979, Cleveland Amory of Fund for Animals led a protest that attracted attention of both kinds—outrage from the sealers and Canadian authorities, cheers from animal defenders. Fund for Animals chartered a ship and sailed up into the arctic waters where the seals were, and one dark night eight young men volunteers from the ship sneaked out onto the ice in temperatures of thirty degrees below zero and painted nearly four hundred pure white baby seals with harmless red dye that made their pelts useless to the hunters. The Canadian police arrived in helicopters and arrested the eight and took them off to jail. As Amory later said, "It's against the law in Canada to do anything to a baby seal except club it to death."

Some people claimed that the poor sealers would be deprived of their livelihood if sealing were ended, but the seal hunts are once-a-year events for which the men earn only about $230 each. Seal hunting is not their regular occupation. The pelts are not very valuable; they are too soft to be made into coats and are used for gloves, toys, knickknacks.

Another widespread misunderstanding is the notion that fur farms are humane and therefore wearing a "ranch-raised" fur is not perpetuating cruelty. In fact, fur farms are businesses where small animals such as minks are kept their entire short lives in tiny indoor cages. They are killed by electrocution, suffocation (with their heads stuffed in jars containing a few drops of chloroform), or their backs are broken. A fur ranch or farm is hardly a farm—it could be in a building on the busiest corner of a city.

The so-called "fun furs" are growing in popularity, especially among young people. They include bobcat, lynx, coyote, muskrat, raccoon, skunk—furs that are less costly than, say, mink, sable, or ermine. Thanks to the fur industry, 106,000 bobcats and 2,300 lynxes were taken in one recent year, and these animals may now be threatened with extinction. At least two animal protection groups, Fund for Animals and Defenders of Wildlife, have petitioned to have bobcats and lynxes put on the endangered species list, which would make selling their pelts illegal.

"What difference does it make if a species becomes extinct?" people sometimes ask. "Except that a species is interesting or people like the looks of it, does it really harm us if a species disappears in the wild? After all, the dinosaurs died out, and lots of other animals have become extinct, and the world didn't end."

When a person asks me that, I usually answer by quoting Dr. Lee Talbot, a leading environmentalist.

Whose Wildlife? Hunting and Trapping 63

Talbot explains that each wild species contributes to the health and stability of the ecosystem it's a part of. When one species disappears, the effects are felt throughout the ecosystem, and some kind of pressure—large or small—is put on every other animal, plant, or insect that lives in that ecosystem. "Wild animals are the indicators of what's coming," Talbot says. "They reflect the health of the habitat and the way we manage our environment. What's not good for an endangered species is usually not good for us either."

It is estimated that a couple of thousand years ago, one species disappeared every fifty-five years. Today, the rate is one a year. We don't know just why the dinosaurs disappeared. But we know that human beings are the major instrument of extinction now.

Joe and Lars returned from the woods after a while. "I found motorbike tracks near the trap site," said Joe. "I think the person who set the trap biked into our woods. I can't believe we didn't hear it." Those bikes make a terrible racket and tear up the land. They're as bad as snowmobiles when it comes to ruining the habitat of many ground-dwelling animals, and in a way they're worse because they can go places a snowmobile can't.

Joe had a cup of coffee to warm up, and then he put the trap in the truck and set off for the village again. A few of the teen-agers in our area have those motorbikes, but we know most of them, and some of them are friends of ours. It seemed so unlikely that one of them would have biked on our land, much less trapped there.

Joe showed the trap to Charlie Vollmer, the local sheriff, and swore to him that from now on we would shoot anyone we found trespassing, but Charlie knows us too well to believe that. Charlie was sympathetic, but he just shrugged when Joe asked him if he had any idea whose trap it might be.

Then Joe drove to the high school and met some of the kids we know coming out of school. Joe showed them the trap, told them about the fox and the motorbike tracks. The youngsters didn't say anything, but Joe got the impression that they suspected who might be responsible. Joe noticed a couple of them exchanging glances.

"There must be someone around these parts who just doesn't understand what Nora and I are all about," Joe said. "If you have any idea who might have done it, I wish you would tell them how we feel about wildlife and ask whoever it is if they would please respect us enough not to hunt or trap or even bike on our land."

The kids nodded. As a matter of fact, most of the young folks around here visit us—they come to see the animals, and to drink the apple cider and eat the homemade cookies we give them. More importantly, we often hire them to help around the place. I think Joe's talk with the young people did more good than calling the game warden, who probably couldn't have done anything about tracing the owner of the trap.

The problem with the injured fox was to hold him long enough for his leg to heal without overly distressing him by keeping him in captivity. When he woke up and found himself confined to the box stall in our barn, he was undoubtedly frightened. We carried food and water to him while he was still unable to stand, but our presence made him so nervous that we didn't stay around.

Whose Wildlife? Hunting and Trapping 65

After a few days, we noticed he could stand and walk. So early one morning, as the sun's thin winter rays were glistening on the frost on our meadow, Joe slipped out to the barn, opened both the barn door and the door to the fox's stall, and quickly came back into the house. I kept the dogs inside with me. Joe and I watched from a window, and pretty soon the fox came warily out the door, looked around, and then limped off as fast as he could toward the woods. The last we saw of him was the white tip of his bushy red tail moving fast through the tall dry grasses.

In the evening, especially in winter, we look out our window and occasionally see a deer or two nibbling on the bushes in the meadow or at the edge of the lawn.

"If it weren't for the hunters, the deer would overbreed the territory available to them and starve to death," goes a familiar argument.

However, people concerned with wildlife know full well that an overabundance of deer is carefully arranged for the sake of hunters. It is no coincidence that there is always a good supply of animals that hunters like to hunt. This is called "game management" or "wildlife management." Those animals that are the natural predators of game animals have been systematically killed off, and the land is manipulated—open land is allowed to revert to brush, thick forest is burned to encourage new tender growth, areas are flooded, and so forth—in such a way as to assure a surplus of huntable animals. (Never mind how this land manipulation may disadvantage or destroy non-game animals—they apparently don't matter.)

Most wildlife experts agree that where the balance of

nature is not disturbed, you rarely find excess numbers of any one kind of animal within a given area. Nature, you must remember, is not humane—nature is efficient. If a certain species begins to overbreed its habitat, only the stronger members will survive. They take the available food, they aren't weakened by any prevalent diseases, and they escape the predators. By the way, that's another unfortunate aspect of hunting: sport hunters always seek the strongest, biggest, handsomest animals, whereas natural predators take the weaklings. Natural predators tend to help keep a species strong.

If sport hunters and game managers really wanted to keep the deer population low to prevent the poor animals from starving, as some of them claim, they would concentrate on killing the females. Yet the killing of does is strictly regulated—to assure a surplus of deer the following year, for hunters to hunt.

The appetite of people for killing animals is nowhere more ugly than in the private "hunting parks" to which animals are brought and released to serve as targets for hunters who pay admission to get in. There was one instance in a hunting park on an island in Florida that will give you an idea of what these places are like. About two dozen lions, tigers, jaguars, leopards, and cougars ("surplus" from zoos, no doubt) were taken to the island in cages that were hidden around the island. People paid $1,600 to get in on this "hunt." As the hunters approached the cages, the doors opened by mechanical releases. But instead of letting the animals get out and run, which would have at least required some skill on the part of the hunters to track and kill them, most of the hunters simply shot the animals while they were still in the cages or just climbing out. So much for the brave big-game hunters.

Once last year Joe was walking at the far end of a field on our property when a deer came crashing out of the woods, stumbling and bumping into trees, and collapsed. Joe could see an arrow sticking into her. She must have traveled a long way and lost a lot of blood, because she was so far gone she couldn't even move when he approached her, but just lay there breathing hard with her tongue hanging out. There was no point in calling Alvin this time. Joe loaded a bullet in the .22 and put her out of her pain with a shot in the head. (In fact, the only reason we have a gun in the first place is for times like this, which fortunately are rare.)

Bow-and-arrow hunters make gun hunters look humane by comparison. Few of them are good enough shots to kill an animal outright; most of them simply mortally injure the animals they hit. Bow-and-arrow hunters are cautioned not to yell after they've made a hit or the animal will run into the woods and they'll have a hard time catching it. The animals run as far as they can with the arrows sticking in them, and then die slow deaths from loss of blood or gangrene infections.

"Hunting is OK because we always eat what we kill." That's another argument Joe and I often hear. Except for deer and duck or pheasant, most game animals and birds are not very tasty, so I am inclined to doubt this. And unless a family desperately needs to supplement its food supply by hunting and would otherwise go hungry, I'm afraid I don't buy this argument from people who can afford to buy their food. We meet some of the biggest local hunters loading up in the supermarket, so few of them are hunting against hunger.

Some people believe hunting is something inborn in human beings. But scientists have spent years studying human nature, and they can't agree on which traits are inborn and which are learned. Since there are vastly many more people who do not hunt than do, it seems unlikely that the wish to shoot animals is a human instinct.

Joe and I know the game managers in our state. They are all farmers or sport hunters themselves—there are no representatives from conservation or humane groups among them. This is true throughout the country. It's well to remember that the wildlife agencies of most states are financed by the money they receive from hunting, trapping, and fishing licenses—so you can see where their interests and sympathies lie. Organizations professing to be concerned with the welfare of animals, such as the National Wildlife Federation, reflect their point of view.

I once heard a wildlife management official talking at a town meeting. "The hunter faces what many of us feel is his biggest threat," this fellow said, "and that threat is the illogical, biologically ignorant, militant-without-good-cause, neosentimental, naive, misled, and too often politically motivated *anti-hunter*." I don't think he was unusual. My experience has been that this is the way wildlife management professionals think.

Wildlife belongs to everybody in this country, and wildlife agencies are supposed to protect the animals and serve the public equally. There are 20 million hunters in

Whose Wildlife? Hunting and Trapping 69

the United States, but over 200 million nonhunters. Yet somehow the public lands seem to be at the disposal of the hunters.

I remember the first time I told an audience of junior-high schoolers about the hunting and trapping that's done in our state parks, state forests, and national wildlife refuges. I noticed many of them were looking puzzled, and then one young man raised his hand.

"Do you mean people can hunt and trap in *wildlife refuges*?" he asked.

Most people think a wildlife refuge is a place where animals are protected from being hunted and trapped. Yet, three-quarters of a million animals and birds are legally killed in these "refuges" every year.

The figures for animals killed on wildlife refuges aren't much, though, compared to the national average. In a single hunting season, the death toll is close to 170 million deer, elk, antelope, bear, squirrel, rabbit, duck, goose, and other birds.

Hunters and trappers aren't the only ones who get special privileges with something that belongs to all of us. Out West, the sheep and cattle ranchers are killing wolves and coyotes on public lands because these animals prey on their sheep and cattle. The ranchers are allowed to pasture their flocks and herds on the land for very low fees. The Bureau of Land Management agents, who are supposed to be protecting our public land and all the wildlife on it, are local people who see things the same way their neighbors do. So they permit and even help the cattlemen and sheep growers to trap, hunt, and poison the wolves and coyotes. At public expense, they also round up what's left of the wild horses and burros because these animals eat the meager forage that the ranchers want for their own animals.

One trouble with our present government system of environment management is that it emphasizes huntable species to the detriment of other species in an ecosystem. The system even introduces stocks of wild animals into areas that are not their natural habitat—just for the pleasure of hunters. One humane organization, Friends of Animals, is waging a strong fight to get the Department of the Interior to change this policy.

We need to insist that government agencies stop manipulating our wilderness areas and state and national forests and parklands for the benefit of the hunting industry and act on their mandate to protect wildlife and assure the healthy survival of all species within a given ecosystem. This should be done so that we and future generations will be able to enjoy wild animals, and because wild animals have a right to a share of the planet.

Studies have shown that most people in the United States would like stronger gun controls. The reason we don't have them is that the powerful hunting industry and various gun associations such as the National Rifle Association are afraid that legal limits on firearms would harm their industry, so they manage to persuade our legislators to vote against controls. The hunting industry, which includes not only guns but all the gear and equipment that goes along with the "sport," amounts to some $2 billion a year. It's almost laughable when you think that ordinary people like Joe and I, along with animal activists everywhere, are fighting against such a huge industry.

The vast majority of people in America have nothing to gain from the practice of hunting. In fact, we have a lot to lose—the destruction of our wilderness areas and the loss of millions of animals that many of us wish to preserve. The way things are going right now, things don't look good for wild animals—unless we animal defenders win the fight to protect them.

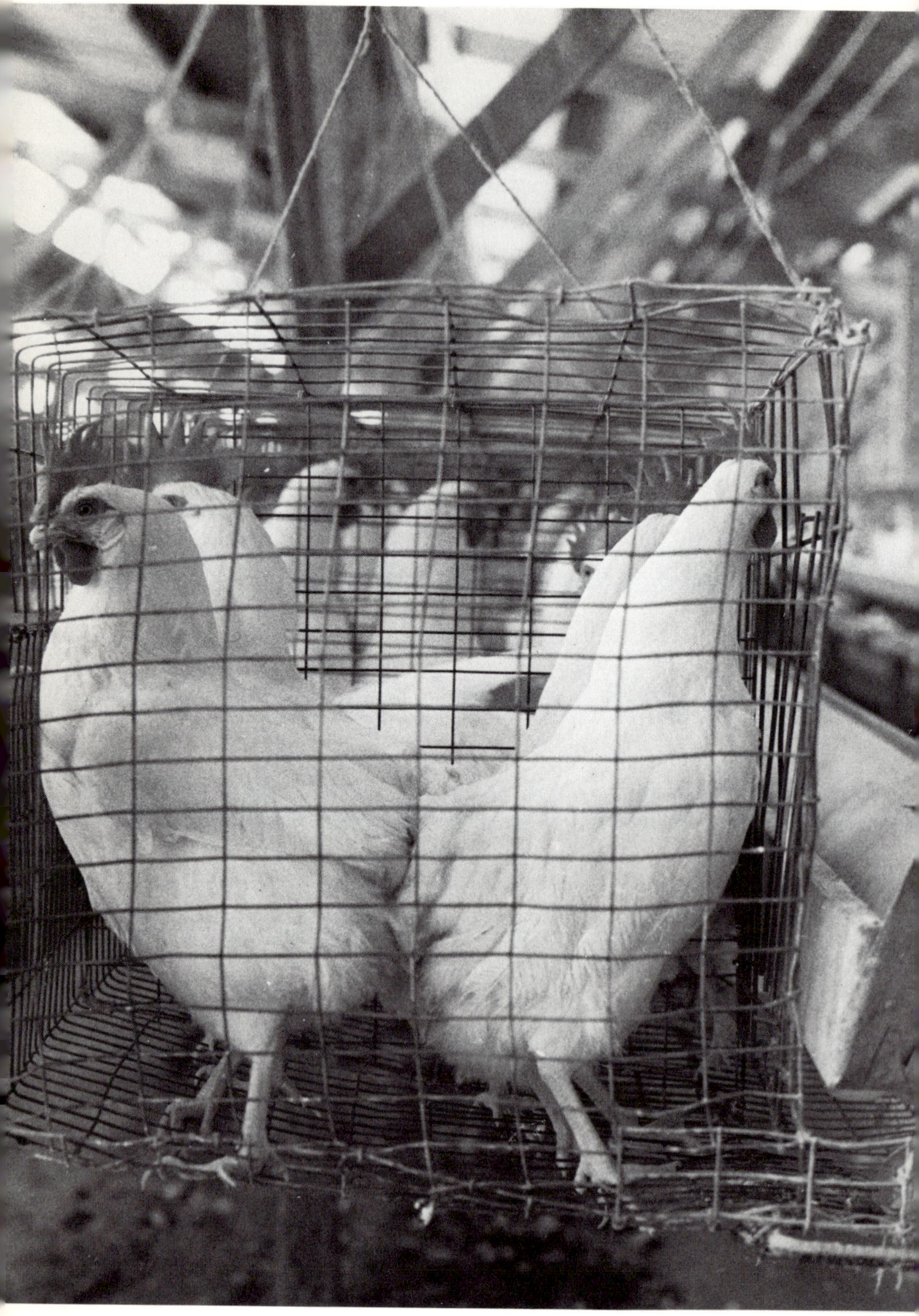

5

WE ARE WHAT WE EAT: Factory Farming

Jennifer McNair is a veterinarian.

I WAS about seven years old and on a routine visit to a farm with my grandfather, the veterinarian in the small farming community in Missouri where I grew up. I wasn't allowed in the stalls where Grandpa was treating some dairy cows, so I was hanging around the hog pen gazing at a litter of brand-new piglets. They were rooting around the mother pig, waiting for her to lie down so they could nurse, when I noticed one little pink pig sort of stumbling on his feet. He couldn't seem to walk straight. When the sow finally did lie down, the other baby pigs crowded in to feed, pushing each other and squealing, but this one little pig didn't seem strong enough to shove his way in among the others and find a teat to nurse on.

"What's wrong with that little pig?" I remember asking the farmhand as he was coming out of the barn.

"Oh, he must be the runt—he may have been born defective, or maybe the sow rolled on him," he told me.

The more I watched, the more upset I got. My grandfather came out of the barn, rolling down the sleeves of his rugged work shirt. "Come along, Jenny, let's go home now," he said to me.

"Grandpa, can't you help that little pig?" I asked urgently, pointing to the runt. "He can't walk straight and can't get any milk."

My grandfather examined the pig, then shook his head. "I don't think that one is going to make it."

I began to cry. "Can't I take him home? I could take care of him and feed him from a bottle and maybe he'd get well," I begged.

"Jenny, he won't live. He's in bad shape. He looks too small and weak to survive," my grandfather explained patiently. "And if he's been injured, he won't mend. I think his pelvis may be broken. If he was born that way, Nature didn't intend for him to live long."

Still I wouldn't move from the fence by the hog pen. I remember feeling this terrible compassion for the pitiful little pig. Just then the farmer came out. When he saw me and heard what I wanted, he said to my grandfather, "Oh, let her take the pig, Doc. He won't pull through, so he's no use to me."

So the baby pig was lifted from the pen and handed to me. I wrapped him in my sweater and climbed into my grandfather's big old car with the pig in my arms.

When we got to my house, which was just down the road from my grandparents', Grandpa fixed up a box in the basement for Peewee, as I had named him. He put some clean rags in, and then took a light bulb on a wire hook and secured it across the top of the deep box so that it warmed the interior like an incubator. Meanwhile my mother gave me an old baby bottle and I warmed some milk. Peewee drank eagerly—he was really hungry. I stayed with him until my bedtime, and left the light on all night to keep him warm.

First thing the next morning, I rushed down to the basement to see how Peewee was. He seemed alert and hungry, but he obviously still had something wrong with his hindquarters. He walked crazily and had diarrhea. I cleaned him up, changed his box, and fed him again.

I spent most of that day with Peewee but toward evening he seemed to grow weak. During the night he died. I cried—both out of sorrow for the little pig and also from a sense of failure. I had really believed, in spite of what my grandfather and parents had warned me, that I could save that pig's life.

I learned from that experience. Human beings, no matter how capable and well-intentioned, have to work within their limitations. You have to accept these limitations. But also, it's good to give a worthwhile idea a try, even against the odds. Peewee had been given some hours of warmth and food and comfort. I wasn't sorry I had done my best for him.

I spent a great deal of time with my grandfather. As I grew older, he let me go along with him on many of his calls. I loved to watch him with the animals—he was so sure and gentle. He did what he had to do, even if it hurt them sometimes, but he treated them with such kindness and respect. He was always urging his farmer clients to do things for their animals that simply made them more comfortable and happy, as well as healthier.

I used to watch him struggling to help a cow with a difficult birth, and I loved to see him rejoice, after hours of hard work, when he succeeded in delivering a living calf. "There you are, old girl," he would say to the exhausted but relieved cow, petting her. "Have a look at your fine baby there." And she would begin to nuzzle the calf in the straw at her feet.

When Gramps lost an animal, we would drive home in silence.

By the time I was in my teens, I was a strong kid and a pretty experienced veterinary assistant. I know I was a help to my grandfather. I could hold a calf or foal while he gave an injection, I could bundle a cat or restrain a dog properly, I could hand him the right instruments for whatever he did, and I assisted in any surgery he did in a barn or field.

Grandpa would never allow me near when he was examining or treating a horse or cow in a stall, though. "Too dangerous," he would say. "One kick in close quarters and you could get your brains bashed in."

Nevertheless, I assumed I would become a vet and maybe work with my grandfather, or at least live in the country and take care of horses and cows, farm dogs and cats, pretty much the way he did. Little did I imagine the kind of work I would wind up doing as a veterinarian. I didn't change my girlhood dream, but farming changed. It wasn't until after I graduated and answered a job ad in an agricultural magazine that I saw one of the farms that practices intensive agriculture.

In terms of sheer numbers, more farm animals suffer than any other animals in the United States—more than homeless strays, more than animals imprisoned in terrible zoos, more than animals used for laboratory research, more than animals abused for sport or entertainment, more than wild animals that are trapped, hunted, and driven from their habitat.

If you drive out into the countryside in most any part of the United States today, you will still see cows and sheep in pastures, hogs in pens, maybe even a few chickens scratching in the barnyards. Yet most Americans do not connect the meat they eat with living animals—it is "beef" not cow, "veal" not calf, "pork" not pig, etc. If they think at all about the origins of the red, well-wrapped pieces of meat they buy in supermarkets, they assume it comes from animals they see on traditional farms.

It does not. Virtually all the poultry and most of the meat we eat comes from huge factory farms where millions of animals live out their short lives confined in environmentally controlled buildings and tended by machines. They are kept in cramped or crowded cages, stalls, or pens, without ever being able to move about normally, groom themselves, exercise any natural instincts, or even see daylight. They are fed unnatural foods, given chemicals, drugs, and antibiotics, and forced to fatten or reproduce quickly so that the farm companies can make money and keep ahead of rising costs. This is called intensive agriculture or factory farming.

It is also called agribusiness. "Farming These Days Is a Lot Like Running a Small Corporation," says a headline in a major business newspaper—and animals are the machines. Of the 145 million animals and 3 billion birds we Americans eat every year, 70 percent of the animals and 98 percent of the chickens are raised in the confinement system. In fact, 80 percent of all agriculture products sold are raised by 17 percent of farms—the big factory farms, of course.

Let me tell you about factory farming and then you'll understand why the days of veterinarians like my grandfather are numbered.

Let's take pigs as they live today on a typical factory farm. After the mother is artificially impregnated, she and several hundred other sows are confined, alone or many together, in small indoor stalls or pens in a large building with a slatted floor over a pit that collects the animals' wastes. (When the pit fills up, it is emptied mechanically.) The sows are fed by automatic feeders.

About a week or two before her piglets are due, the mother is moved to a farrowing building, where she is put in a stall so small she can barely move. She might even be tethered or strapped down to keep her from rolling on her young as they are born. Normally, if a sow rolls on one of her babies, it squeals and she hears it and gets up. But in the farrowing building, the noise is so great that a sow can't tell the voices of her own piglets, so she might lie on one without noticing.

A few weeks after the piglets are born, they are removed from their mother, placed in tiny pens, and fed grain, with antibiotics mixed in, by an automatic feeder. Soon they are moved to small slatted-floor pens in a nursery building. The mother is bred again to produce more baby pigs, like a machine. She might also be given hormones to synchronize her fertility and make her produce piglets at a time convenient for the farm managers.

After a few weeks in the nursery, the piglets go to "finishing" pens—in another building on the same farm, or perhaps on another farm that specializes in finishing. During finishing, the pigs are crowded together so tightly they are pressed right against one another, hobbling on concrete, metal, or plastic slatted floors slippery with excrement. Because they are so stressed by the crowding, some of the pigs bite each other or the bars of their stalls in frustration. (Formerly, pigs in these pens would bite one another's tails off and become infected, so to prevent this, the pigs' tails are amputated before they are put in finishing pens.) They are usually fed by automatic feeder. They are continually given antibiotics, either in their feed or by injection. In four to six months, the pigs are shipped to market and then to slaughter.

In other words, most pigs today lead their entire lives in total close confinement, with no relief, ever. Because of this, these normally clean and rather intelligent animals suffer greatly from stress. Their instinctive behavior is completely distorted.

Intensive agriculture has revolutionized farming. The confinement system reduces some of the problems that my grandfather's farmer clients had to deal with. For example, exposure to certain animal diseases is minimized by confinement. On the other hand, factory farming has its price, too. Because the confinement causes such stress in the animals, they are highly susceptible to a whole spectrum of stress-related diseases. So the farmers must rely on ever-increasing amounts of drugs and antibiotics. Think about that the next time you eat a pork chop. Beef cattle are routinely fed hormones to make them fatten faster, right up to a week or two before slaughter. Think about that the next time you eat a hamburger.

I often wonder if some of the farmers miss the contact they used to have with their animals. My grandfather always used to marvel at the knowledge some of his clients had of their horses or cows, even their pigs, goats, or sheep. They knew their animals' quirks and habits, their personalities. My grandfather always said some farmers knew their cows better than they knew their wives.

I remember the way the little calves would follow their mothers, and the way the cows in the pasture would quietly try to stand between you and their babies. The first time I saw calves on a factory farm, I could hardly believe it.

A day or so after birth, a calf is taken from the cow and placed in one of perhaps hundreds of stalls in rows in a darkened barn. The stall is so small that the animal can barely lie down but not turn around; it is usually tethered at the neck, to restrict it even further. The entire building is kept in darkness most of the time to further discourage the animals from trying to move.

The calves are fed milk only—you'll see it on a menu as "milk-fed baby veal." This diet produces anemia (iron deficiency) in the animal, which accounts for the nice white color of veal. The animals often instinctively try to lick and chew parts of their stalls in an attempt to get roughage and iron. They are given no hay to lie on

We Are What We Eat: Factory Farming

because hay contains iron. They also lick and chew parts of their bodies because they are crazed by the immobility and monotony of their existence.

At least 10 percent of the calves die during the confinement period. The rest are given an array of antibiotics and drugs to ward off diseases that this restraint and inadequate diet make the animals susceptible to. In a few months, they are slaughtered.

The animals that suffer perhaps most of all are layer chickens. A chick emerges from its shell in a tray in a hatchery. If the hatchery is in the business of producing egg-laying hens, the tiny male chicks are quickly sorted out and dropped into plastic bags to suffocate. The toes and tip of the upper beaks of the female chicks are cut off so they can't peck or scratch each other later on when they are crowded together in stressful conditions that would make them fight each other.

They are then sent to a "grow-out" building and kept mostly in darkness for twenty weeks till they are mature enough to go to an automated layer house. Here the young hens are confined, several together, in wire cages so small that many of them soon cannot move at all. They are kept in semidarkness to quiet them and to stimulate laying. They are fed and watered by conveyor belts. After about a year of continual laying, the hens are worn out, so they are killed and made into chicken soup or pet food.

Chicks destined to become broilers, on the other hand, are taken to the broiler house within a day or two of hatching. The tips of their upper beaks are cut off, their toes clipped, and they're put under warm lights to stimulate feeding. Then they spend their eight-week life span on the floor of the broiler house with perhaps 25,000 other birds. Their legs wither from lack of exercise.

To eliminate the necessity of catching each chicken separately to slaughter it, researchers are working on mechanized systems that would drop the birds onto conveyor belts or suck them up from the floor into giant "harvesting" machines.

Some scientists are concerned with the effects that this kind of farming, with its reliance on growth hormones and antibiotics, might have on human health. And there is no question but that the stress those billions of animals suffer brings about the release of hormones which change their body chemistry. What effects do all these chemical and hormonal changes have on us when we eat the flesh of these animals? Certainly we are eating deranged and neurotic animals; whether or not this can harm us is unknown.

There was an interesting belief among some American Indians—I am reminded of it in this connection. They considered it unthinkable to eat a deer that had been hunted and killed in a way that had terrorized it and made it suffer, because they believed they would be taking the animal's fear into themselves!

One thing is sure—factory-farmed meat is less nutritious than meat from animals that can move about. Lack of exercise makes animals put on fat that's high in cholesterol.

Other scientists are questioning the waste of food and energy that our American high-meat diet costs. Our meat animals consume more protein than they produce.

Only about 5 percent of the food that is poured into the mouth of a cow in intensive agriculture is returned as meat. Even a little broiler chicken, the most "efficient" factory animal in terms of yield for effort and money involved, returns only about 22 percent of the protein in its feed in the form of meat. In the future, as the world's population increases, this will not turn out to be practical if we are going to avoid world starvation.

And still other scientists are beginning to be concerned about polluting effects of these vast agribusinesses. The waste materials of these billions of animals are filled with chemicals. Will these be harmful as they accumulate in our land and water?

You may ask what all this has to do with me. What can I do about all this, as a vet? Well, I am interested in our environment, in pollution, in matters of food production and diet and world hunger. But my main interest is in the animals caught up in—in fact, created for—this huge food-production industry. Right now I am employed on the staff of a humane organization, trying to have some influence on today's livestock methods and to get legislation passed to help farm animals. I think my job as a veterinarian is to defend animals. In the case of factory farming, I think the treatment of the animals must be examined for many reasons—not the least of which is the cruelty involved.

I know that humane considerations are considered unscientific. Goodness knows we weren't taught anything about them in the veterinary school I attended. But there is certainly a job to be done on behalf of the animals in the factory-farm system.

I don't blame the small farmers—in fact, factory farming has put most small farmers out of business. They simply can't compete against the huge corporate farms. Veterinarians who work for these big producers are on the spot, too, because their livelihood depends on them. So the animals get trapped in this cost-profits squeeze. And there's very little public concern for their suffering. Even people who care greatly for their pets, or who become incensed at the slaughter of baby seals, can be surprisingly indifferent to the plight of meat animals.

Part of my work as a scientist is doing research aimed at finding practical alternatives to the factory system. But until we come up with a substitute that is both humane and economically attractive, I try to find ways to relieve the pain of factory-farm animals. I also try to create ways to reduce small farmers' costs so they can be economically competitive with factory farms.

Sometimes I help draft practical animal protection bills that some legislators are willing to sponsor, and work to get them passed. A few countries in Europe—Sweden, Denmark, West Germany, for example—already have some laws to protect factory-farm animals. One suggestion that still remains to be put into law, anywhere, is that each animal should be able, without difficulty, to: 1) get up, 2) lie down, 3) groom itself normally, 4) turn around, and 5) stretch its limbs. That does not seem like too much to ask, does it?

Once recently I spoke in Congress before a joint hearing on agriculture problems. I told the senators and representatives some of the things I've been telling you about, and showed them slides. Their reactions were interesting. Some of them got up and walked out before I was halfway through my presentation—they just couldn't handle it. Others were simply stunned.

"I had no idea this is the way meat animals are raised," said one fellow—and he was from a state where there's a great deal of factory farming!

People from humane organizations have to be careful when making speeches in public, especially when trying to influence lawmakers or the courts. We are always in danger of being accused of being sentimental or of distorting facts out of sympathy for animals or some such. I make it my business to be very well informed and not to exaggerate—just tell the facts and show the pictures, even when I'm boiling inside. I think I get through to people better that way.

Talk about lack of awareness, I run up against it all the time—especially when I campaign to make kosher slaughter included under the humane slaughter laws. The Humane Slaughter Act of 1958 requires that an animal be rendered unconscious before it is hoisted up by its hind leg and bled out. Slaughterhouse workers are supposed to use a captive-bolt pistol to stun each animal. However, ritual slaughter requires that an animal be conscious when it is killed, and so at present, kosher slaughterhouses are exempt from federal and state humane slaughter laws.

"What do you mean, it's cruel?" Jewish people ask me. "Kosher slaughter is one of the most humane methods of killing an animal—when its throat is slit, it quickly loses consciousness."

When ritual slaughter took place in the old days, the

conscious animal was confined on the ground in what is called a casting box, and its throat was cut with a very sharp knife by the *shoichet*—a man who by tradition was supposed to be a skilled wielder of the knife. The Torah, or book of Jewish law, intended ritual slaughter to be humane. I assume an animal with a properly slit throat does lose consciousness rapidly.

However, when certain sanitation laws were passed in the United States in 1906, animals could no longer be on the ground when killed. The custom of hoisting and shackling animals for slaughter was born. So what happens in kosher slaughterhouses is that fully conscious animals are hoisted up by one leg and their heads secured against the wall by iron hooks put through their nostrils while they await the knife of the *shoichet*. Heavy steers will twist and struggle in their agony, often breaking their legs and tearing tendons. And animals are not hoisted and slaughtered quickly, one at a time. A long row of animals is hoisted and shackled, and then the *shoichet* comes in and does his work. Many frantic animals hang there waiting in excruciating pain for a long time until the *shoichet* gets to them. The bellowing of the shackled animals is unbelievable.

Some Jewish people who are involved in animal protection are strongly against this method of kosher slaughter, and are trying to get changes made to end the animals' suffering. This is a humane, not a religious, issue.

The Humane Slaughter Act was extended in 1978 to cover more slaughterhouses than it did originally. While better than nothing, it still should be strengthened. The Department of Agriculture agents who are charged with inspecting slaughterhouses and enforcing the law can't be everywhere and they have limited powers, and many slaughterhouse workers are careless or indifferent.

Some people object so strongly to the killing and eating of animals that they become vegetarians. Some vegetarians will eat fish, some not. Some don't even eat eggs or dairy products such as milk and cheese—these people call themselves vegans. Many vegetarians and vegans are reluctant to wear leather and are hard-pressed to find good shoes and boots made of synthetic materials.

People who find vegetarianism difficult often seek out meat and especially dairy products that they are assured come from free-ranging, unconfined animals. Some health-food stores can be trusted for this, some not; it's best to ask questions and do a little research so you don't get ripped off.

Not all vegetarians are animal sympathizers—thousands of people eat no meat because they believe meat is harmful to their health. There is a great deal of nutritional and medical evidence that our typical American high-meat diet is not good for us, and that we would be healthier if we ate more whole grains, vegetables, and fruits. But it seems to me unlikely that everybody in our country can be persuaded to stop eating meat any time soon. Therefore, though I am a vegetarian myself, in my work I do not try to convert people to vegetarianism. Instead I concentrate on helping animals through what I think we can achieve right now—better laws, more information, humane changes in intensive agriculture.

One of the most important aspects of my work is simply making people aware of the way animals are raised, shipped, and slaughtered in order to put meat and other animal products on our tables. Sometimes I speak at schools and colleges and urge young people to ask questions, become active, and make choices for themselves about the matter of eating animals.

One action that could be taken at once might be to have animal products labeled according to how the animal was raised, shipped, and slaughtered. Then we could buy animal products that are certified to have come from nonfactory sources. Perhaps they would be more expensive, but the extra cost for humaneness would be worth it.

In Framingham, Massachusetts, the MSPCA (Massachusetts Society for the Prevention of Cruelty to Animals) is developing a model farm that will not only give an historical perspective on farming in America but will raise some live animals and—most importantly, to me—will have exhibits that show modern intensive livestock production and methods of handling and transporting animals. The visitors to Macomber Farm are in for a shock, I bet. But I think projects such as this will go a long way toward helping people examine their priorities in selecting their diets. And Macomber Farm will make compassionate people aware of an area that has long been overlooked in the struggle to improve the lives of animals and to relieve their suffering at the hands of people.

Wouldn't I prefer to be working in direct contact with animals, taking care of horses, cows, and cute little calves as my grandfather used to do? Yes, I would rather do that eventually. I enjoy visiting my friend Ned, a small-animal vet in a nearby suburb. Last time I was in

Ned's clinic, a family brought in a beautiful golden retriever named Dandelion, a great pet, who was extremely sick with an abdominal infection. Helping Ned examine and treat the dog, and seeing the family's relief when he told them she was going to be okay—well, that's really rewarding. But for now, I would like to effect some changes in the factory-farming system. There is a need for scientists with my training and experience. If I can help get some laws passed to relieve the poor cows, calves, pigs, and chickens, then I'll open my own practice and start taking care of patients.

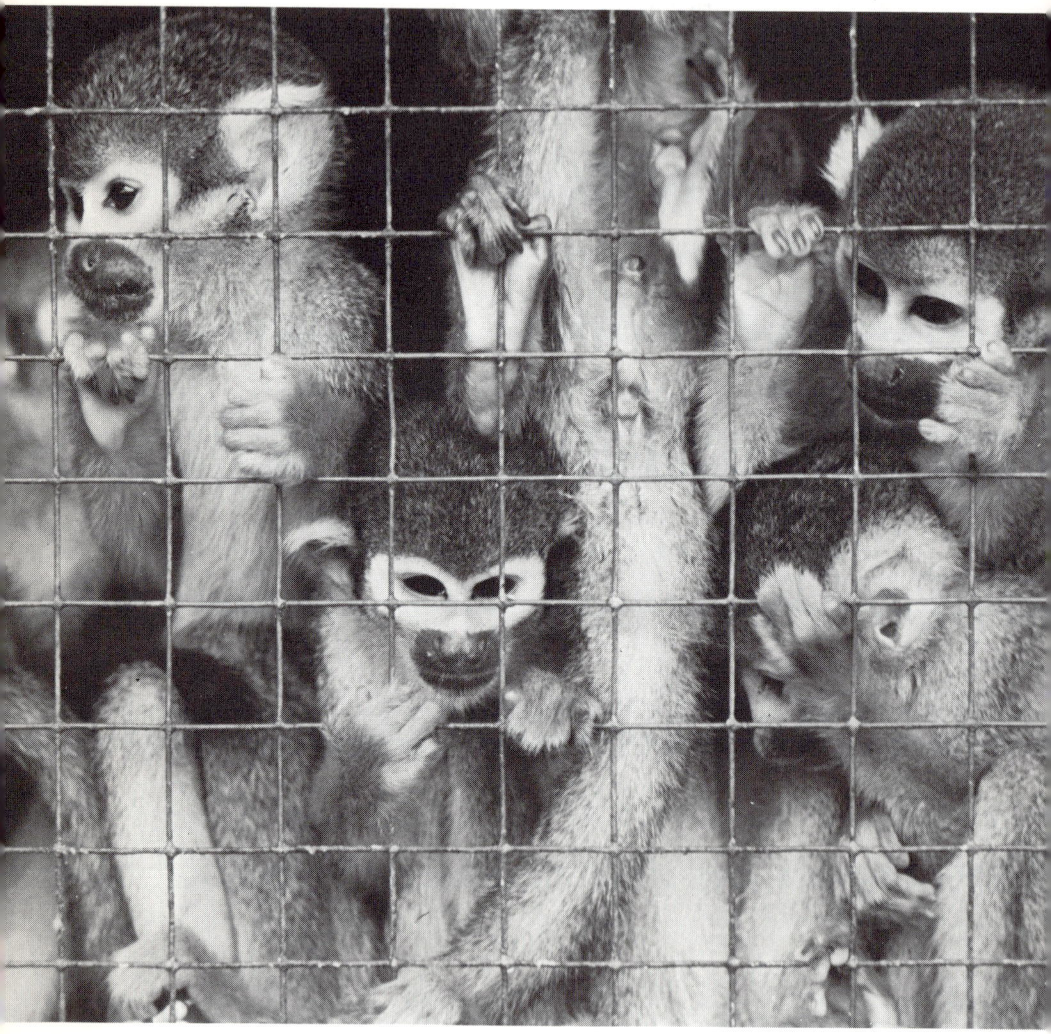

6

PRISONS OR HAVENS?
A Look at Zoos

Gary Williams is a curator of mammals at a large zoo.

ABOUT a year after I started working at the zoo, our city finally voted some funds for improvements. I had been making a study of the animals that needed help the most, and drawing up proposals for the changes I thought should come first. I wanted to enlarge the pens of some of the animals and make them more like their natural habitats, but I also wanted to put into effect some of the new ideas that had been worked out at a few other zoos by animal-behavior specialists like myself.

One of our first projects was to make an important addition to the cage of our large puma cat, Jake. Jake had a pretty good-sized cage, compared to some I've seen in other zoos. He had rocks to stretch out on in the sun, shrubbery to shade him and give him some privacy, and a cave for shelter. But he had become listless and was losing weight. We have learned that the size of an animal's cage may not be as important as the opportunities it offers for activity. Jake's cage—while it was not one of those bare concrete boxes—afforded him little to do. Jake was suffering from one of the most prevalent illnesses that can afflict caged wild animals: boredom.

Boredom can become a serious physical illness. The minute you trap a wild animal, transport it, put it in a cage, expose it to the daily view of people, and curtail all its normal living habits—roving, chasing, hunting, exploration, play—you put it in a state of stress. The boredom that sets in when an animal has nothing to do all day and night adds to the stress. And stress can affect the entire body of an animal, and make it sick.

We had a plan for Jake that had worked well for pumas and tigers in a few other zoos. We were going to rig up a mechanical system that would make him simulate some of the activity of hunting and capturing his dinner. In the wild, of course, most animals do not eat at regular hours—they hunt and eat when they're hungry, and they spend a large part of their time at it. In a zoo, their food is usually delivered to them regularly, whether they are hungry or not, and without their so much as lifting a paw. You might think an animal would be relieved at not having to work for its dinner, and should be glad to never go hungry. But with many animals—especially the carnivores whose normal food is other creatures instead of plants—that is not the case. They become fat, dull, and lazy and, like Jake, listless.

We laid a little track on the ground that extended from a hole under a rock to another hole about eight feet away. The holes were about thirty feet from a wooden platform where Jake often lay or sharpened his claws.

Then we brought in a toy marmot—a kind of ground squirrel that pumas think are especially tasty. We attached the mechanical marmot to the track, rigged up a mechanism that would activate the marmot when Jake's weight was on the platform, and attached a timer.

The idea was that within about fifteen minutes of the puma's jumping onto the platform, the toy marmot would dart out of one hole and scurry along the track into the other hole. And here's the best part—if Jake pounced fast enough, and scratched around the hole into which the marmot had disappeared, he would press a lever that caused meat to be delivered to him. If Jake was slow on his feet, and the toy marmot disappeared seconds before he got to the hole, nothing would happen. Jake would have to go back to the platform and "stalk" again.

You can see this setup would accomplish three things: It would give Jake something to do, it would give him the exercise of pouncing, and it would let him have control over when he ate.

After we got this thing set up in his cage, we let Jake back in. Do you know, he caught on to the way it worked within a couple of days? He was fascinated by it, and pounced a lot in the beginning. But within a few weeks he got so he would stalk only when he was hungry, and he never left untouched, decaying food lying around his cage the way he used to when he was fed regularly by his keeper. Now it has become less costly to feed him because his food doesn't ever go to waste—so the zoo has saved some money while Jake has become sleek, muscular, and more alert. His speed has improved, too, and now he often catches the "marmot." We have had to replace it several times with a new one, as he sometimes demolishes it. We're working on creating one that will be pounce-proof.

In my first year at the zoo I also spent a good deal of time studying the eating habits of our zoo's servals, those beautiful little spotted cats with unusually long legs. Servals are talented hunters. In the wild, they can flush birds out of the bushes and catch them in the air. It's a sad sight to see zoo servals uninterestedly picking over the food that is slapped down on the floor of their cages every day.

One day I was invited to a special meeting of the zoo's board of directors to introduce my proposals for improving some of the animals' enclosures. I made a little speech about the servals' natural hunting abilities that were withering away from lack of use and about the animals' general apathetic attitude.

"I have a plan for reawakening their natural hunting and capturing abilities," I said to this rather dignified group of people who control the money for the zoo. "I call it flying meatballs."

There was a startled silence. Then a director cleared his throat. "You call it *what*?" he asked. "Mr. Williams, this is no time to joke. We are discussing improvements for the zoo that will cost money and must be worth it."

"I am not joking, sir," I said. "What I am proposing is fastening an apparatus to the top of the serval exhibit from which the meatballs can be dangled and flown back and forth, over the heads of the animals. The animals will leap up and capture their prey, so to speak. The apparatus will make them work a little for their dinner, similar to their natural way of catching their food. I think it will improve their health and preserve some of their agility."

The directors began to smile and ask questions.

Prisons or Havens? A Look at Zoos

"How will you know the appropriate height for the meatballs?" asked one. "It wouldn't be fair to exhaust the animals every time they wanted food."

"My assistants and I have worked out the height based on their size and on studies of distances they can easily leap horizontally," I answered. "We also know that these particular servals eat in a rigid hierarchy with very little competition for food among them. They take turns, each animal eating a little and then waiting till its turn comes around again. We believe the flying meatballs will improve the animals greatly."

"All right, we'll consider it," said a director. And sure enough, the board included money for this project in our budget.

Not only did the animals perk up and seem to enjoy their flying meatballs, but they got exercise they had never gotten before. The animals began to make fantastic leaps to capture their "prey." And there is an additional bonus—the public, which up till then had simply gazed at several unusual cats lying about in their cage, now gets to see a little of what a serval is all about! You should hear the oh's and ah's from the crowd around their cage when the servals are catching their dinner.

You have probably seen zoo bears pacing back and forth in their cages, shaking their heads from side to side. This is not normal behavior for bears; it is a sign of boredom and stress. We rigged up a way of letting our polar bears "order" their fish over a microphone in their cage when they are hungry. Instead of a bucket of fish being spilled onto the floor of the bears' cage every day, fish are delivered directly into their tank when the bears vocalize certain sounds which the microphone picks up. The bears have to dive in and get the fish, just as they do in their natural habitat. After we initiated this means of letting the bears have some control over their lives—namely, eating when they are hungry and "capturing" their food—their health and appearance improved greatly, and they stopped their constant pacing. One of our bears, a male, put on some weight, even with the additional exercise he gets from diving into the pool. And again—this activity is fun for the public to watch.

One improvement we made didn't cost the zoo anything but made a noticeable difference to our two macaques. Macaques are large monkeys that forage on the ground for their food. In the past, the keeper just emptied a bucket of food into their large concrete cage every day—which is the way most captive animals get their food, unfortunately. But now the keeper strews the animals' fruits, vegetables, roots, and seeds around the cage and then covers the food with a thin layer of hay. The macaques can forage for their food, and it gives them something to do. They seem to be much happier monkeys now; the keeper has commented on the change that has come over them. Because this made more work for the keeper, we assigned a student volunteer to help him part time. The student doesn't go into animal cages, but helps out by loading the food onto wheelbarrows, bringing it to the exhibits, and doing other chores.

These kinds of innovations could be made by any zoo, at little or no cost, to relieve the misery and monotony of caged animals' lives. New zoos especially offer the opportunity to put into practice our knowledge of the needs of animals. I've heard there is a new zoo in the Pan-

Prisons or Havens? A Look at Zoos

aewa Rainforest in Hawaii with such naturalistic habitats for the animals as a swamp for the tigers and an island with vines for the gibbons to swing on, and abundant seclusion for all. But most of the 180 zoos in the United States are little more than prisons for animals. Millions of people stare at zoo animals without realizing the stress and suffering that characterizes the lives of most of them.

Take a cheetah, for example, a beautiful animal and superb hunter capable of running 60 miles an hour. People can look at one lying stupefied with defeat and frustration in a sterile, ten-foot concrete cage—and not think anything about it. It isn't that people are cruel or indifferent—most people who go to zoos like animals. It's just that they aren't aware of what they are really seeing. Some humane groups, such as Friends of Animals and the Society for Animal Rights, work hard to try to expose the terrible conditions that many zoo animals have to endure.

Worst of all are the vicious little roadside zoos, where a few half-dead beasts are caged in squalid misery. But even in zoos that have spacious pens for the animals, many of the creatures are sickly and stressed. Captivity carries with it a whole host of threats, especially to mammals and birds: being constantly on view to the public; unfamiliar, unnatural, and unvarying food; restricted movement; crowding; and bare cages. Sometimes just a difference in climate or environment can literally kill an animal. And some captive wild animals die from just plain homesickness.

Today, most zoo animals have been born and bred

in captivity. This is preferable to the hunting and capture of wild animals, which is a violent business, carried out by men who are not famous for their compassion. The capture of baby chimpanzees and other primates is especially brutal. The hunters have to kill the mothers and usually others of the wild ape colony in order to capture the infants.

Even with all the hunting and trapping that wipes out wild animals, the greatest threat to them is loss of habitat. As cities and towns grow, and more and more wilderness is taken over by human beings for their own use, the living space of wild animals is shrinking rapidly. Every year more species are added to the endangered list.

The English author Gerald Durrell founded and runs his own beautiful small zoo on the island of Jersey in the English Channel, just to preserve endangered species in an environment as humane and naturalistic as possible. Cages are designed to provide hiding places, companionship, and plenty of "toys"—branches, pools, and opportunity for digging or for dismantling things for animals that get their fun that way.

"Since you're depriving an animal of territory, you must provide it with an adequate substitute or you'll have a bored, sick animal on your hands," Durrell comments.

I think zoos can be havens for the wild animals of the world. The trouble is that most zoos continue in the terrible tradition of the old-fashioned menagerie—as places of amusement for people. Zoos should be transformed into parks where groups of the same species can maintain themselves and the public is kept at some distance.

Prisons or Havens? A Look at Zoos

Instead of attempting to have as many different kinds of animals as possible, to amuse the public, good zoos today are concentrating on having larger numbers of fewer species. Animals will be healthier, behave more normally, and will be more likely to reproduce successfully if they can live with sizable groups of their own kind and have both privacy and space to move about. A few zoos in some areas of the United States are also concentrating on keeping only the animals that do well in their particular climates, rather than trying to force many different species to adjust to climates that are alien to their natures.

Zoo professionals today are working on two special problems: encouraging certain species to mate, and keeping newborn infants alive. In the past, if a living infant was born in a zoo, the mother would often either deliberately kill it or neglect it. Zoo personnel would sometimes succeed in getting the baby out of the cage and raising it, but on the whole this was not successful. Too many were lost.

Now we know a little more about the habits and needs of captive wild animals. For instance, we've learned that the males of some species like to have some pretend combat with other males before they feel like mating. This is true of some primates, such as macaque monkeys, and also of many of the hoofed animals—deer and goats. We have also learned that the females of some species need complete isolation—not just from the public but from other animals—when they give birth and nurse their young. Polar bears and certain kinds of wolves are like this. But among other animals—fennec foxes, for example, and those little golden monkeys called marmosets—

an isolated mother has a poor chance of success in giving birth to and raising living young. Among these species, the nursing mother likes to leave her young from time to time and mingle with the others. And with these animals, the males also participate in rearing the young, so the opportunity for this should be provided.

Some animals have to learn to be mothers—it isn't always something that just comes naturally. We now know that the marmosets have to learn from their own mothers and help take care of younger brothers and sisters before they can successfully raise their own young.

Some of our better zoos have their own vast breeding farms. The San Diego Zoo's Wild Animal Park covers 1,800 acres and has areas that look like the savannahs of Africa. The National Zoo's Research and Conservation Center at Front Royal, Virginia, is not even open to the public, and the scientists try to be as discreet as possible so as not to frighten or disturb the animals.

We had some real excitement in our zoo last year when two baby gorillas were born. Gorilla births are relatively rare in zoos. In the past, gorillas have usually refused to breed in captivity. Considering the way these gentle, sensitive, shy and intelligent beasts are kept in most zoos even today—demented and dispirited in bare, cramped concrete cages with no privacy—it is not surprising that their normal mating and nurturing instincts have been so distorted that they either refuse to mate or the mothers neglect or kill their babies. Infant abuse, which happens only occasionally in the wild, is common among zoo and laboratory primates.

At our zoo, a small colony of gorillas is kept in a

Prisons or Havens? A Look at Zoos

large compound that is as naturalistic as we could arrange, with lots of bushes and grasses to give the animals both privacy and places to explore. They are under the devoted care of a highly competent young keeper named Susan.

One morning I ran into Susan as she walked from the canteen, looking rather disheveled and carrying a paper cup of coffee.

"How's Kuba?" I asked her, referring to the gorilla that I knew was about to deliver.

"I think she'll be going into labor any minute," said Susan. "I slept near the compound all night because I don't want to miss the birth."

In the past, Kuba would have been isolated as her time approached. Susan, along with our veterinarian and a primate consultant, had decided to leave her with the others. We knew that another gorilla colony had had a much better experience when they left the mothers in the group. Kuba herself had been born in captivity, and her mother had had one other offspring before Kuba was bought by our zoo when she was four years old. We were all wondering if she would know what to do with her baby.

Our gorilla group consisted of a dominant male, three females, and a young male that was so respectful of the older male that they all lived harmoniously. Needless to say, we hoped that harmony would continue when our first highly valuable gorilla infants were born.

Susan stayed near Kuba's compound all that day; I brought her a sandwich and a Coke toward evening. Kuba was behaving normally—in fact, she seemed to be hungry and was searching the ground for leftovers from their earlier feeding. I had no sooner left Susan than she gave a little shout.

"Gary! Come quick!"

I ran back down the path to the gorilla compound. Kuba was indeed in labor—attended by the other two interested females, who actually seemed to be encouraging and supportive. Within fifteen minutes she delivered a male infant. Susan and I were quietly delighted and fascinated. Kuba was busy taking care of business. Then about an hour later, Bert, the giant male, walked over, and we held our breath.

"Boy, if he harms this baby, we're in trouble," whispered one of the attendants who had joined us.

"I'm sure he won't," Susan whispered back.

Sure enough, the huge animal looked closely at the baby, and then, ever so gently, touched it. Kuba made no move to stop him or run away. She had cleaned her baby and now held it to her breast. Susan, of course, was ecstatic, and we were all jubilant that things were going so well.

But the best was yet to come. When Priscilla, the other pregnant female, gave birth ten days later, at first she seemed surprised and confused by her infant. She appeared very nervous, but when Kuba sat down beside her, she seemed to calm down. However, Priscilla didn't seem to know how to handle her baby. When she held it to her breast, she held it upside down. She couldn't place it on her back correctly, piggy-back style. She seemed all thumbs.

What was so interesting was that Kuba actually

appeared to teach her, even to correct her when she did something the wrong way. The two mothers and their babies spent nearly all their time together, and we never did have to take either baby away and raise it by hand on a bottle, which was common practice a few years ago in any zoo lucky enough to have a live gorilla birth.

I remember an incident that happened when I was a teen-ager which strongly influenced my decision to go into zoo work.

My family was visiting in a southern city that had a rather pretty zoo, and I used to spend most of my days there. I became especially interested in an exhibit of capuchin monkeys. They lived in a very large enclosure that contained plants and small trees so they could swing and climb. But the first day I was there, I noticed a little female that seemed not to be accepted by the others. They chased and harassed her, and at feeding times they wouldn't let her get to the food. If she managed to sneak up and grab a piece of food, the others zoomed after her, screaming, until she dropped the food in fright or a pursuing monkey took it away from her.

As the days went by, I became more and more concerned and even spoke to one of the keepers about her plight.

"Oh, she's new," he said indifferently. "They'll get used to her after a while." I doubted it. Even though I was still a kid, I knew enough about animals to realize that the little female should be rescued from that cage. She was literally trapped and in danger, and she showed it—daily she became more thin and anxious. The memory of this little monkey haunted me for months, even years.

At the end of each year, zoos have to report to the Department of Agriculture all deaths of animals and the causes of death. After I entered zoo work professionally, I had occasion to go through some zoo reports. Just out of curiosity, I checked the report from that particular zoo for the year when I had seen the monkey tormented by her cage mates. Sure enough, the zoo reported the death of a female capuchin monkey. Cause of death? Starvation! In one of our country's better zoos, an animal's ordeal was ignored and the creature was allowed to starve to death.

While nutritional deficiencies, infectious diseases such as tuberculosis, and parasites kill many captive animals, the leading cause of death is injury. It seems unlikely, doesn't it, that animals in cages or pens would have much opportunity to hurt themselves. But they get hurt through badly designed and poorly maintained cages or pens, they hurt one another, and they mutilate themselves in their boredom. Zoo animals, for instance, have been known to chew themselves or to lick parts of their bodies raw. Quarreling and picking on smaller, weaker, or newer animals account for losses, too—like the little capuchin monkey I saw.

Zoo animals are also insufficiently protected from the public. The number of animals that die yearly from foreign objects thrown into their cages or from actual slaughter by vandals is one of the most shameful statistics in zoo-keeping. This happens because there are too few guards, or because of careless and negligent guards. It is hard enough on an animal to be in captivity, even under adequate conditions. To expose a captive animal to an

Prisons or Havens? A Look at Zoos

enemy—people—when it is trapped in a cage and can't get away is criminal.

And in one particular way, some zoos actually permit people to harm their animals—in the so-called petting zoos. Petting zoos are those in which children are invited to handle the animals—usually baby animals. (Some petting zoos remove all the teeth from the animals they turn children loose on.) The idea is, I suppose, that this will attract support of the public for the zoo. Maybe people even imagine these zoos will teach children something about animals. Such zoos often display an infant chimp or monkey dressed up in human baby clothes and nursing from a baby bottle. What this spectacle teaches children about the true nature of these fascinating animals is difficult to see.

Even those zoos that have optimistically put only baby farm animals in petting zoos cannot afford the close supervision necessary to keep small visitors from maiming, teasing, and tormenting the animals. The argument goes that domestic farm animals will not suffer the way wild animals would, but exposing any animal to crowds of children is cruel. I'm glad to say our zoo does not have a petting zoo.

One of my colleagues, John Lukens, works with aquatic mammals in a small "seaquarium." In his care are a beluga or white whale, three dolphins, several seals, and a pair of killer whales named Gramp and Orky.

The survival rate for most sea mammals in captivity is not very impressive, John says, for the same reasons that so many other zoo animals die. They suffer from injuries, parasites, infections, malnutrition, and of course stress. I suppose it's hard for the public to believe marine mammals feel imprisoned in those huge tanks of water they are kept in, but remember that these animals are used to a huge ocean world—deep as well as broad—and the tanks where they are confined must seem even smaller to them than enclosures or cages seem to zoo animals.

One thing John does for his sea animals is check their water regularly to make sure the filter is working properly. His animals are kept in clean, filtered seawater. Some sea mammals in other zoos are not so lucky—they are kept in dirty water with either no salt or with the wrong amount of salt, which subjects them to infections and skin problems.

Gramp and Orky are something to see—handsome, graceful animals nearly thirty feet long. They perform beautiful underwater ballets and are friendly enough to allow John to get into their tank with them and ride on their backs. Killer whales, or orcas (their true name), are among the most misunderstood of marine animals. Some rinkydink places advertise them as "ferocious, dangerous, man-eaters, etc." Actually, while they are flesh-eaters and in the wild hunt efficiently in groups for small whales, seals, and dolphins, they are friendly to human beings and highly tamable. Most of the performing whales you see at marine parks are killer whales.

The biggest problem with newly captured marine animals is getting them to eat. John says we are just beginning to understand their natural diets. In the future, as our oceans become more polluted, these small marine animals will probably become as threatened with extinction as the larger whales are.

Many compassionate people today believe that zoos are so inhumane and the conditions the animals must endure are so deplorable that zoos should be phased out completely. They point out that a wild animal in a zoo is so stressed that it is genetically altered within a few generations and therefore it is no longer the same animal that it was in the wild. Skeletal changes occur due to lack of the exercise animals in the wild normally get from chasing and being chased. Why put animals through the torture of imprisonment, these people ask, when the species preserved by zoos are drastically changed and not the real thing? I have to admit that judging by what I have seen of most zoos in this country and abroad, they are right.

However, zoos don't have to be prisons for animals. They can be set up in ways that I have been telling you about, so that the world's wild creatures can be saved from extinction without causing them to suffer or to lose their wild capabilities. In my opinion, there is no way to save our larger wildlife species except in zoos or preserves. We need to rebuild and improve our zoos, change them into naturalistic, animated environments where people can get a glimpse of the many marvelous forms of life on our planet and appreciate their unique behaviors.

Art museums are places where the art treasures of the past and present are protected and preserved for us to be inspired by and learn from. Why can't zoos be set up and managed in the same spirit, not as places of amusement but as museums where the living treasures of the world are protected and preserved, both because we enjoy them and learn from them and because they have the right to continue?

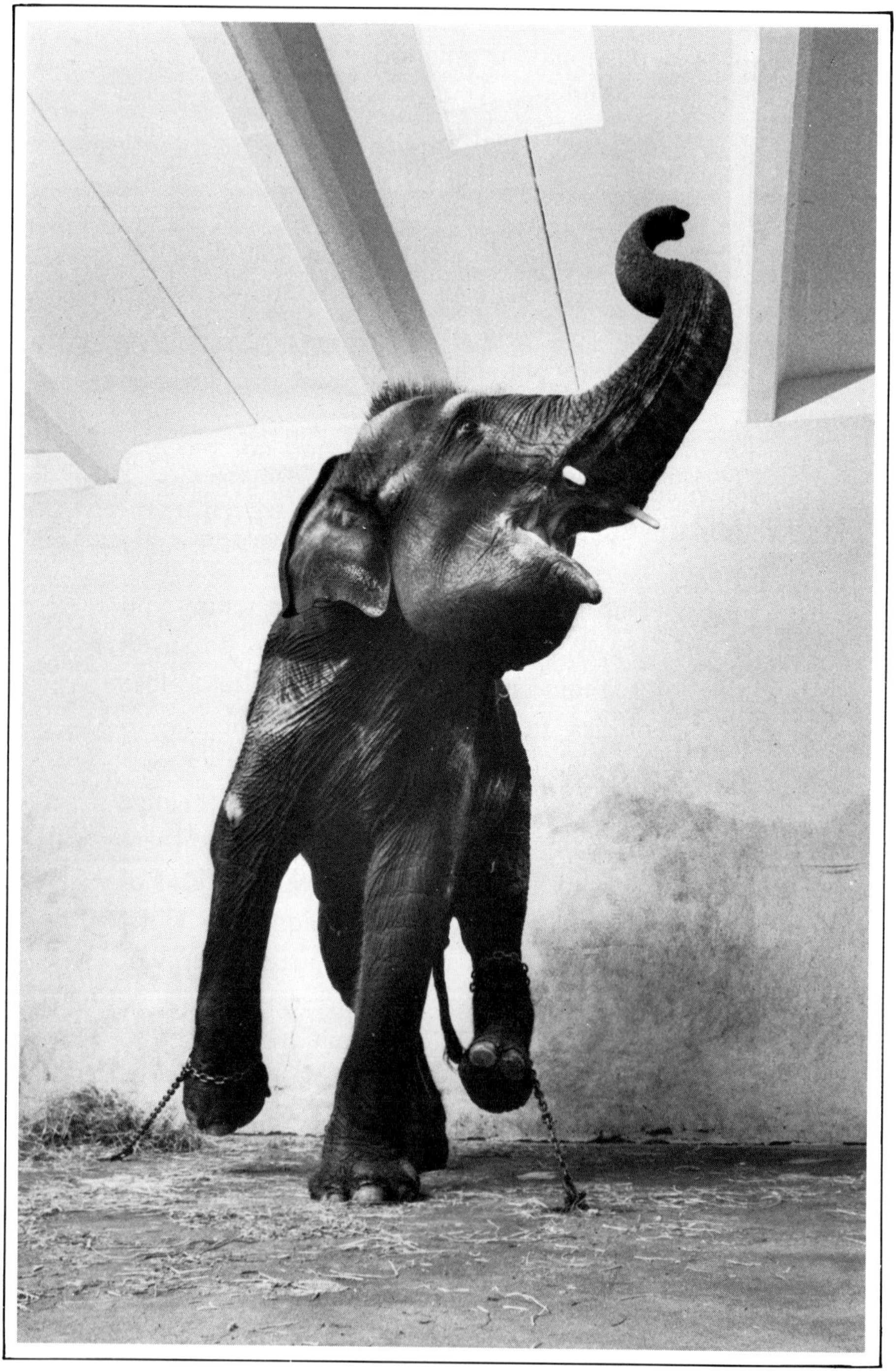

7

RIDE 'EM, COWBOY!
The Use of Animals for Entertainment

Jeff Alexander heads
a law enforcement division of the ASPCA.

THE movie crew with all its gear had already gathered on the street when I got there. The cameras and sound equipment were ready, and in spite of the fact that it was early on a Saturday morning, a sizable crowd of spectators hung around on the edge of the activity, watching.

The wet cobblestone streets glistened from the recent rainstorm. A man led a horse out of a van and stood in the street, holding it by the bridle. Another man put a Western saddle on it. Pretty soon the star of the movie, a well-known actor, walked over, followed by the director and several others of the crew. The actor circled the horse, looking it over. That's when I walked up to the director and held out my identification badge.

"I'm Jeff Alexander from the ASPCA," I said,

taking care to be very polite. "Could you tell me what kind of scene you're going to use the horse in?"

The director, a middle-aged bearded man wearing dark glasses, glanced at me, then turned away brusquely. "Talk to this guy, will you, Mike?" he asked one of his assistants and walked off to consult with his chief cameraman.

The assistant explained to me, rather condescendingly, that the star of the picture was going to gallop down the street, jump off the horse in front of one of the buildings, and tie the horse to a railing. I picked up one of the horse's hooves and looked at it.

"This horse is not properly shod for galloping on this street," I pointed out. "It could very easily slip on the wet cobblestones and fall and break a leg."

"Look, we've rented this horse, and those are the shoes he came with," said the assistant, getting annoyed.

"Well, I'm very sorry, but if you force the horse to gallop on this street wearing those shoes, you're breaking the law," I said firmly.

The film assistant stared. "You've got to be kidding. You're not going to try to prevent us from shooting this scene? Do you know what this is costing us?"

"I am not kidding," I replied. "Look—it's not only for the horse, it's also for your actor's sake. If the horse falls at a full gallop, the actor could get hurt."

"What's holding us up?" asked the director, returning. This time he spoke directly to me. "What's the problem?"

"You either have to get proper shoes on this horse so he won't fall on the street and break a leg and maybe break your star's neck," I explained, "or else you can't ride him at a gallop. It's as simple as that."

"Look, we're losing time," said the director, reaching for his wallet. "Can't we settle this?" Some people think money will solve everything.

By this time, others of the film crew had come over and were hanging around, listening with interest. I guess nothing like this had happened before—possibly other riding scenes had been shot out in the country on dirt roads.

Just then the actor returned and swung himself into the saddle. "This horse seems fine to me. I'm ready—let's go."

I was beginning to get disgusted with these dudes.

"Sir," I said, "if you ride this horse, I'm going to have to arrest you."

The actor frowned, but before he could say anything, another member of the crew spoke to the director. "Look, this could turn out to be more trouble than it's worth," he said quietly. "Maybe the guy is right. We don't want Bob to get hurt. Let's look at the schedule—we can shoot around this scene now, and send the horse back to the stable for different shoes, or call a blacksmith or something. Meanwhile, I'll get a police permit to close off the street for a couple of hours this afternoon to keep the traffic out, and we'll do the horse scene then."

After a little more discussion, it was decided to follow that suggestion. I came back in the afternoon and inspected the horse's shoes again before the riding scene began. This time the horse was wearing rubber-covered metal shoes, which won't slip and slide on wet streets, and the scene was shot without incident. While I was not the most popular person on the scene, I noticed I was treated with a grudging respect. For me, it wasn't a power trip—it was my job.

The use of animals in movie making has long been a matter of concern to animal welfare people. In the interest of realism, terrible cruelty to animals, including death, is commonplace in filmmaking. I was successful in the incident I told you about because I work in New York State where the ASPCA has the authority to enforce the state laws that protect horses and other animals. But in most places in the United States and in other countries, there are no such laws—or if there are, they are not enforced—to protect animals from the atrocities done to them in the name of the filmmaker's art.

Animals are filmed attacking and killing other animals, they are brutalized into fighting people, they are killed in hunting scenes, set on fire, pushed over cliffs, disemboweled, shot, and treated to just about every torture you can imagine. All this is duly recorded on film by the movie makers to add realism, excitement, and spine-tingling horror for the entertainment of the movie-going public.

These cruelties are not only reported by humane organizations who protest whenever and wherever possible, they are also reported by film actors and actresses themselves. Some who are animal lovers have formed an organization called Actors and Others for Animals, with TV star Earl Holliman as its head.

The situation with animals in movies is so acute that

for some years humane activists in California, including Actors and Others for Animals, have been trying to get a law passed that would prevent the motion picture companies from abusing animals and would also prohibit them from distributing films made elsewhere that showed the tripping, wounding, mutilation, torture, or killing of animals.

"I've been in 187 films, and I know whereof I speak when I say the animals desperately need this protection," said one veteran actor.

Among the worst abuses is the brutal practice of horse tripping, which is commonplace in Westerns. You must have seen plenty of movie scenes in which a horse running at full gallop suddenly falls head over heels as the Indian—or the cowboy, gunslinger, member of the posse, or whoever—riding the horse is "shot." Horses are often terribly hurt or even killed in those falls. The tripping is done with a rope controlled by the rider, who is always an experienced stunt man. Humane groups are rarely able to prevent any of this.

Another wealthy industry in which animals are cruelly used for entertainment is the multimillion-dollar Western rodeo business. The public thinks the "bucking bronco" events consist of spirited, ornery broncos ridden by brave cowboys. In fact, the animals are just regular horses who are in severe pain, and most of the riders are trained, well-paid professional athletes. The reason the horses thrash about is that a bucking strap is pulled tightly around their genitals where it will hurt the most. In its pain, the horse bucks hysterically, trying to rid itself of the strap. And the reason horses and bulls come roaring wildly out of the chute is that they have been given an "assist" with an electric prod. When running calves are roped and slammed to the ground, they are often badly hurt and sometimes their necks are broken.

Since I've been a professional humane-organization worker, I've become aware that the cruelties in the use of animals for sport and entertainment are widespread. Take horse racing, for instance. It's true that the horses, if they are big money winners, are well-fed and cared for. But the commonplace, legal practice of injecting a horse before a race with Butazoladin, a drug that reduces inflammation and pain, makes it possible to get a lame or injured horse to run. The animal does not feel the pain during the race, but it may break its leg or become a hopeless cripple.

According to members of horse-protection organizations, including some horse veterinarians, no horse two years old or under should be running a race at all—its bones are not yet strong enough to stand the strain. That is why every now and then you see or read about a young race horse whose legs have simply snapped in the middle of a race. A sizable number of young horses break down, never becoming winning thoroughbreds, and have to be retired or killed. It is surprising that the owners nevertheless continue to take the chance and put them in races anyway, but of course there is big money involved if they win.

Some owners of show horses seem to be more concerned than race-horse owners about their animals' health and safety, except for Tennessee Walking Horse owners, who often "sore" their animals before a show. *Soring* means injuring a horse's front feet so they hurt; the horse

Ride 'Em, Cowboy! The Use of Animals for Entertainment   115

will pick them up high and try to walk with its weight on its hind legs. This fancy way of walking is one of the characteristics on which this breed is judged, so usually the sorest horse, not the best one, wins. Thanks to the efforts of the American Horse Protection Association, an active organization devoted to fighting cruel practices against horses, soring is now illegal—but it still goes on in many instances because owners have learned to sore their horses' feet in such a way that it doesn't show. When inspectors from the Department of Agriculture, which enforces the law against soring, catch a case, they fine the owner. Trouble is, the fine isn't very big, and there aren't enough conscientious inspectors to catch all the violations.

Greyhound racing has never been the wealthy industry that horse racing is, and in fact it is illegal in most states—not because the state officials are too kindhearted to permit such a mean sport, but because it attracts underworld gamblers. On the other hand, some states—including my own—are now beginning to toy with the idea of legalizing greyhound racing as a source of badly needed revenue through the taxes it would bring in.

Greyhounds lead sad, muzzled, businesslike lives; they are not treated as pets. If they don't race well they are either killed or sold to research labs. I've never seen a race, but I've seen these poor animals when they're shipped through New York's animal port on their way from one state to another. And while it is supposedly illegal to use live rabbits as a lure in the actual races, live rabbits or kittens are used in the training of the dogs. The small animals are tied, dangling and squealing, onto a lure frame just ahead of the dogs. To encourage the young dogs, they are allowed to take a bite now and then until the bait is dead.

"Sometimes we have to use three or four rabbits in the course of a day," I once heard a trainer complain.

Animal protection organizations such as the ASPCA, the Humane Society of the United States, and the Fund for Animals have waged war on greyhound racing for years. But some people believe it may be dangerous to oppose greyhound racing publicly, ever since a newspaper reporter investigating crime in Arizona (a state where greyhound racing is legal) was murdered by a greyhound breeder.

Except for California, all our states ban bullfighting. A few years ago, an enterprising promoter hit on the idea of staging a bullfight on a huge barge that was to be towed out and anchored off the Atlantic coast, beyond the territorial limits, where he couldn't be arrested. Following a tip, I had gone undercover to this fellow's office and bought a couple of tickets to the fight, which furnished the proof I needed to get an arrest warrant for him. We caught up with him standing on a corner of Fifth Avenue with the matador—can you believe he was holding a press conference? What a character. We arrested him on the spot. The bullfight never came off.

California's legal bullfights are supposed to be bloodless, and held only as part of religious festivals. The bulls are not stuck with the sharp lances used in Mexican and Spanish bullfighting, and they are not killed. Animal welfare groups oppose these fights anyway because the animals are taunted and teased for the amusement of the crowds; these groups fear the fights will lead to legalization of the ritual torment and slaughter that characterizes regular bullfighting.

Because fights between animals are prohibited in many states, such savage contests as dogfights and cockfights are held secretly. They are illegal in New York, but sometimes we get a tip that a cockfight is going to take place, and then my job calls for real detective work.

First, because these fights are usually held at night in rough neighborhoods, I make sure I have an assistant and a few plainclothes policemen lurking nearby when we go on a raid. Finding the exact place where the fight will take place is always hard because they change the location several times, right up till the last minute, to throw off law-enforcement agents. I don't try to look like a bettor—they would spot me as a phony right away. I pretend I'm a salesman, selling those razor-sharp spurs that are put on the feet of fighting cocks to enable them to inflict greater harm on each other than just their claws would.

Just as the fight is about to start, we move in. We issue summonses to the men conducting the fights. The crowd, of course, splits in all directions. We confiscate the cocks—they're beautiful animals unless they're too badly scarred. Some are so seriously injured we have to destroy them.

I've never been knifed, beaten up, or threatened, even when I'm undercover by myself trying to locate where a fight will be held, but I must admit sometimes I'm scared. Of course, I can't show it or I'd blow my cover.

Dogfights, also illegal and held in secret, are apparently on the increase in our country. Five years ago it was estimated that there are as many as 40 to 50 breeders of fighting dogs and at least 1,000 fights a year. The "sport" supports two known publications.

While they are still puppies, fighting dogs are trained ("blooded," as dogfighters call it, for obvious reasons) with live kittens and cats. Small-time dogfighters do not use pedigreed, highly bred fighting dogs, but will take ordinary dogs from animal shelters, give them drugs, and work them over with electric prods to make fighters of them. A dogfight sometimes lasts for hours, with severely mutilated and dying animals still showing what their owners proudly call "heart" to fight. One of the contestants is often killed by the other; sometimes neither survives. A dog who tries to run away during a fight is called a "cur" and killed contemptuously.

Humane organizations all over the country have been trying to hold the line against dogfights under each state's laws against gambling. Some states also have humane laws that prohibit fights between animals. The problem is that laws can always be changed. The only real assurance against the legalization of bullfights, dogfights, and cockfights is a public that is not amused by these spectacles.

It is not difficult for an animal lover to look at a rodeo or a dogfight and see that it is extremely cruel to the animals involved. Far more difficult to assess is that beloved spectacle, the circus. I have trouble making some people believe there could be anything wrong with such an innocent show.

You might make a good argument that elephants,

for example, have been domestic animals for thousands of years, and that making them perform is no worse than putting show horses through their paces. Legends exist about the affectionate relationships that are formed between elephants and their handlers and even the people who perform with them. No doubt many of these tales are true.

And yet—evidence suggests these highly intelligent beasts are not always happy, and in fact some are quite crazed from the lives they lead. It is not unusual to read short newspaper stories, tucked away on the inside pages, with headlines such as "Elephant Crushes Its Trainer" or "Circus Elephant Kills Caretaker."

These two headlines were real, and appeared within two months of each other. In the first story, the elephant killed her trainer when he slipped and fell during a performance, suggesting a feud in which the animal was awaiting her chance. The elephant was, of course, instantly shot. Another elephant performing with her was so terrified when it saw what was happening that it escaped, tearing through the tent and fleeing into a nearby forest, where it was cornered and captured, trembling with fear, a few hours later.

In the second report, an elephant was chained to the floor when for some reason her caretaker began to push her in the face and put his hand into her mouth. She stood this for a while, then suddenly picked him up with her trunk and hurled him against a pillar and kicked him.

Sometimes elephants try to escape. While an animal the size of an elephant could not get very far in a large city, apparently they occasionally run away in rural areas. I once read about two circus elephants who escaped to the woods around a country town in Oklahoma and managed to hide out for weeks, eluding search parties consisting of virtually the entire town. I'm inclined to believe that circus elephants are severely stressed.

Similarly, the accounts of trainers who are mauled by big cats raise additional questions in my mind about the feelings of circus animals.

What are we really seeing when we look at a performance of, say, fifteen Bengal tigers sitting on their haunches, ears flattened, snarling, batting their giant paws at a man in a sequin-spangled coat with a prod in one hand and a whip in the other? The true tiger, a four-hundred-pound muscular animal of unsurpassed beauty, virtually extinct in the wild, is by nature a solitary jungle dweller, an efficient hunter, dangerous to man only if injury or old age prevents it from capturing its usual prey. Yet here are a bunch of overweight, churlish cats, some of them toothless, lined up together going through awkward motions for a crowd of spectators. From the looks of them, their trainer is a man of impressive bravery—but true tigers they are not.

Naturalists who know tigers estimate that because of hunting and the dwindling of their habitat, wild tigers are doomed. If we want to see a tiger in the future, we will have to look at an adapted version that can accommodate to zoo living, or else accept these cross and foolish animals in the circus—but let us not kid ourselves that we are seeing tigers.

A good circus with its exciting atmosphere, its spirited music, its fantastic trapeze artists, skillful acrobats, delightful clowns, beautiful performers—how can we take a stand against something that is so much fun? Yet some of the animal acts are very troubling. Maybe it's okay to use cute little costumed dogs, and horses that are certainly treated no worse than other domestic horses. A pair of well-cared-for, broad-backed horses, patient and wonderfully synchronized, galloping around the ring while four or five clever acrobats jump on and off their backs is one thing. But to me, a flabby and toothless lion or tiger prodded out of a cramped cage and forced to jump through a flaming hoop and perform other unnatural stunts is quite another matter.

In addition to the entertainment people derive from animal spectacles such as fights, races, and the like, there's the use of animals for pleasure. Public riding stables and dude ranches fall into that category. My department investigates all the riding stables in our area. The abuse we find most prevalent is the working of horses with open saddle sores. These are usually caused by inexperienced stable hands putting the saddles on wrong so that they rub, and then leaving the saddles on too long, so the rubbed areas become more and more irritated.

Of course, most riders don't notice. We wish that people would refuse to ride horses with open sores, or any other injury or illness, and report the stables to their local humane-law-enforcement agencies.

As for dude ranches, a friend of mine, Robin Kemp, told me a story about something that happened when she was fourteen. It is a good example of what can make someone become an animal activist. Some of us become professionals, like me, but we need people like Robin to help us do our job to protect animals. She can tell her story better than I can.

Robin speaks:
I was touring Colorado one summer with my family on our way to the music festival at Aspen. We live in Massachusetts and had never been in the West before. The plan was to spend a few days at a dude ranch to ride and enjoy the typically Western type of recreation there in the Rocky Mountains—riding, hiking, barbecues, and the like. I was a horse lover and a good rider; I really looked forward to riding out West.

The ranch, an attractive layout in Winter Park, looked appealing—a comfortable lodge, sturdy cabins, stables, corral, outdoor barbecues, the works, all surrounded by pine trees and the mountains rising behind.

As soon as I was settled in my room, I ran out to the corral to look at the horses before dinner. What I saw was a scraggly bunch of about twenty-five emaciated, apathetic animals that were trying to eat the dusty hay piled in one corner of the corral.

"Why are they so thin?" I asked an elderly man in ranch clothes standing nearby.

"They were just brought down from the mountains a few weeks ago," he told me. "They ain't had much to eat."

I didn't know what he meant by "brought down from the mountains."

"They winter on their own up in the high mountains," the man explained. "Would cost too much to feed 'em during the winter when they don't earn their keep.

Ride 'Em, Cowboy! The Use of Animals for Entertainment 123

The ranches become ski lodges then. We don't own these horses—none of the ranches hereabouts own their horses. We all rent 'em from a guy in Boulder. His outfit brings the horses down from the mountains—them that has survived—when the dude ranches open in summer."

I wondered what kind of fun it was going to be to ride one of those poor beasts next day through the steep forests. I had never worried much about the health and comfort of the horses I rode back home. They had always looked pretty well cared for. But these!

Next morning at breakfast, someone asked one of the waiters, "What happened at the corral during the night? We heard a lot of snorting and squealing and commotion."

"I think one of the horses kicked another," he explained. "They sometimes fight at night."

With growing apprehension, my younger brother Mark and I went out to the corral for the morning ride. The horses were saddled and tied to the fence by the barn, all except for one horse that stood alone in the middle of the corral.

"Oh, him, that's Stanley. His leg's broke," said one of the wranglers when I asked. "They was in a fight last night and he got kicked."

I ran out to the horse, who stood with his head drooping and one leg held gingerly. "Has someone called the vet?" I asked. The wranglers gave me a funny look. "I reckon so," said one vaguely and walked away. The owner of the ranch had come out to watch the riders start off; I ran up to him. "The outfit that owns him is going to come and get him," said the owner. But I knew Boulder was a long distance away. "Isn't there a vet nearer here?" I asked. I was aware that in a case like this, the merciful thing would be to have a veterinarian put the horse painlessly to death with an injection, since it is virtually impossible to mend a horse's leg.

Just then one of the wranglers called me. "Let's go, miss. Your horse is over here," he said. I was pretty upset and bewildered, but I went over to him. He was holding the bridle of one of the most pitiful horses I had ever seen. The horse's hip bones stuck up in huge knobs, his back was swayed, and he had a bad wound on his neck. There were patches on his withers where the hair was rubbed off.

"I can't ride that horse," I said miserably. "He looks sick."

The wrangler looked at me impatiently, then went to confer with the owner. The other riders were beginning to get restless. Just then my parents walked up; they had come to see my brother and me ride off. When they saw my horse, my father spoke to the owner.

"My daughter is a good rider—don't you have a better horse? This one really doesn't look as if it should be ridden at all," he said.

A somewhat better horse was produced, and I got on. My dreams of the good riding I had looked forward to in the beautiful Rockies were rapidly disintegrating—and with it my enjoyment of this place. I remember thinking, if this is what dude ranches are like, and if we had known it, we never would have planned to visit one.

Twenty-five riders left the ranch at a walk and headed for the wooded slopes nearby. The little boys among us kept kicking their horses and jerking the reins and shouting, "Giddy-up!"

My brother looked at them with disgust. "Haven't you ever been on a horse before?" he asked another boy about his own age. "You don't flap your arms and kick the horse and pull its head like that. Where do you think you are, on TV?" The other kids just stared at Mark and kept on kicking their poor horses.

The horses struggled up the steep hill behind the ranch with one of the wranglers shouting and urging them on. His costume was right out of a Western movie, right down to the sharp star-shaped spurs. I thought he was a jerk.

At the end of the ride, Stanley was still in the middle of the corral in the hot sun. I asked if he had been given water.

"He can't walk over to the trough," said a wrangler as if he were explaining something obvious to a moron. "How about bringing water to him, then?" I asked. I picked up a bucket, filled it, and carried it to Stanley, who drank gratefully.

By the end of the day, no veterinarian had arrived, but around five o'clock a truck pulled up with another horse, which was unloaded from the crude trailer. The driver looked at Stanley with annoyance.

"Can't you shoot him here like you did that horse that got kicked last week?" he asked the owner. "Why do we have to drive him back to Boulder to do it—he'll fall on the way and maybe bleed from that leg all over the trailer."

The owner glanced at me and a few other guests who

were standing nearby. He seemed angry that the driver had revealed the way Stanley was going to be treated.

I couldn't stand any more and ran up to my room. So out here horses are treated like pieces of equipment, I thought. They're interchangeable. One breaks down and the rental company replaces it. They don't call veterinarians to help the horses. Also, I asked myself, why do these horses fight so much at night? Is it because they are hungry? I remembered the dirty hay with the clouds of dust rising from it.

I told my parents the whole story. They listened sympathetically. Mark chimed in, "I don't like this place. Let's leave."

"Yes, but I want to help these poor horses," I said. "What can we do?" I burst into tears of frustration.

"We'll report this ranch to one of the humane organizations," said my mother firmly. "We'll make a complaint about the condition of these horses, as well as the incident with Stanley. Colorado must have humane laws, and surely this ranch is treating the horses in a way that's against the law."

My family packed up and departed the next morning after breakfast. At the nearest town, we called the Colorado Humane Society and also the American Humane Association in Denver. The officers we spoke to promised to inspect the dude ranch, check on the condition of the horses and suggest that they be properly fed. Both groups can report abuse cases to the Colorado Bureau of Animal Protection, which can initiate legal action. Possibly a citation was drawn up against this ranch.

Looking back, I can understand that, realistically,

it's unlikely that the humane agencies of any western state are going to seriously crack down on dude ranches, because tourism is such a big business and source of income for the state. If the dude ranchers complain that the humane laws hurt their profits, the state enforcement people will probably let up. Nevertheless, perhaps the visit of the humane officers would inspire the owner of that dude ranch in Winter Park to call a veterinarian the next time one of the horses was injured—especially if enough guests were to protest.

I returned home after the summer a lot more mature. My illusions about dude ranches were gone. Furthermore, I was determined to devote part of my life to helping horses such as those I had seen at the ranch. With some of my friends at school, I formed a junior humane organization, dedicated to helping all animals and particularly horses. We kids made it our business to check out all the riding stables in our part of Massachusetts, and we reported some of them to the humane organizations and state humane officials.

One day I read about the American Horse Protection Association and decided to join that, too. I became a junior member along with eight hundred other young horse lovers like myself all over the country. It made me feel good to be a part of a group that was trying to help animals as I wanted so desperately to do. By the time I finished high school, I was already an experienced animal welfare activist, something that has given me satisfaction all my adult life.

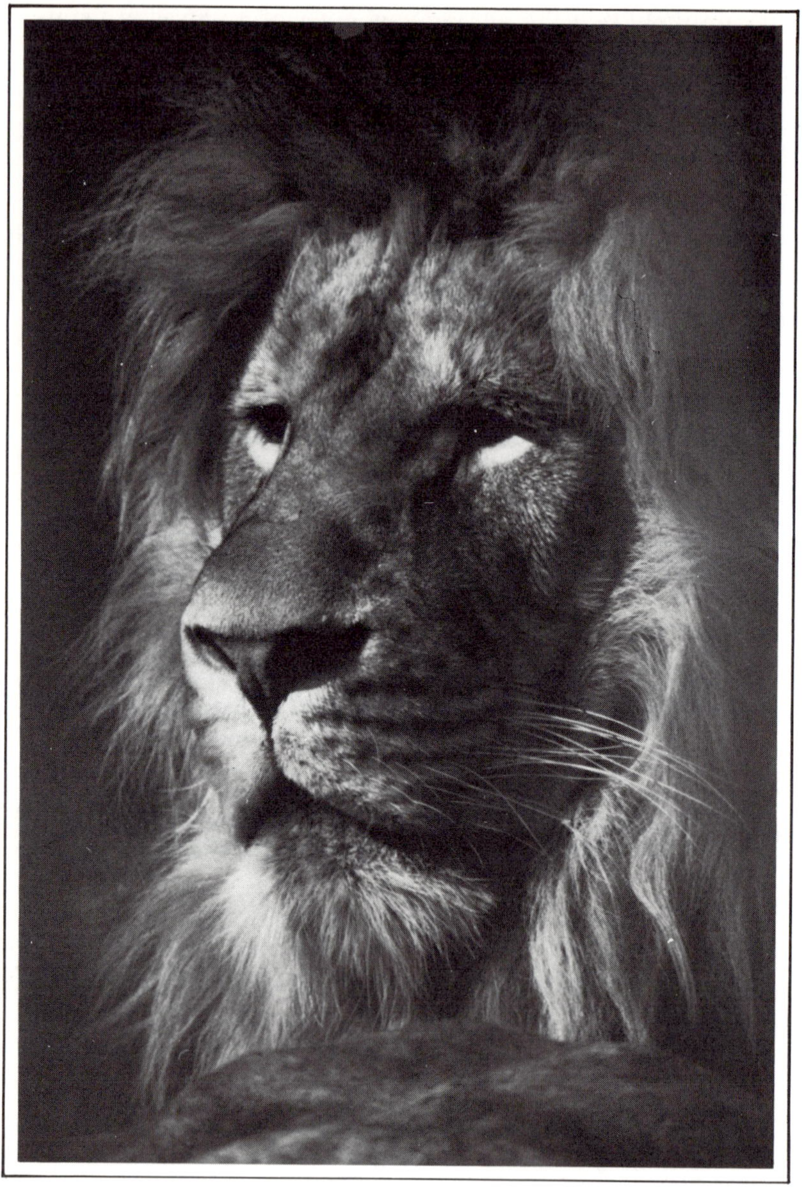

8

Animal Rights

What are the rights of animals?

THE Declaration of Independence speaks of the "unalienable rights" to life, liberty, and the pursuit of happiness with which people are endowed by their Creator. Americans believe human beings are entitled to these rights simply by virtue of being alive. But while people acknowledge that animals undoubtedly have the same Creator, they do not mention the "unalienable rights" of animals.

On the other hand, rights are not the same as laws. Laws serve to define what rights are and to set punishments for those who act against them. In other words, you have the right, let's say, to move about freely and go where you wish, within reason. This is guaranteed by law. But you don't have the right to prevent somebody else from doing the same. If you restrain others, tie them down or lock them up, you can be arrested for it, and, if a jury finds you guilty, you can be put in jail and your right to move about freely will be taken away.

But, in practice, rights are what you get from life, not what the law says. No matter how many or what kind of laws are passed about rights, they don't mean much unless they're translated into behavior. If the people in our society don't recognize and support animal rights, the laws won't do animals very much good.

From very early times, human beings have felt certain obligations and duties toward the animals they subjugated. Hundreds of years B.C., philosophers and scholars were arguing about whether or not animals could think and whether or not they had souls, but most agreed that animals were entitled to a certain amount of kindness. In Biblical times, people apparently treated their domestic animals—sheep, goats, oxen, donkeys—with a sort of casual kindness that was more or less taken for granted. While neither Testament of the Bible contains much in the way of specific injunctions against cruelty to animals, many religious scholars believe kindness to them is implied in Judeo-Christian principles. These scholars say that if you are a good Christian or Jew, you will automatically be compassionate toward animals.

The first laws in America that acknowledged the rights of animals were the anticruelty statutes of the Massachusetts Bay Colony in 1641. "No man shall exercise any Tirranny or Cruelty towards any bruite Creature which are usually kept for man's use," said the Puritans, and persons who violated this law were apparently prosecuted.

Most people are not aware of the laws already in existence that give legal rights to animals. New York enacted the first state law to protect animals in 1828, making it a misdemeanor to mistreat any *owned* horses, cattle, or sheep. It took nearly a hundred years, but all the various other states eventually followed with anticruelty laws. Arizona was last, in 1913.

The first federal animal protection law was the Twenty-Eight-Hour law, passed in 1873 and replaced with a stronger law in 1906. It concerned the transportation by ship and railroad of cattle, sheep, and swine. The law mandates that during their long journeys, which were in unbelievably horrible conditions, the animals had to be given food, water, and rest every twenty-eight hours.

In the mid-1950s, a few American meat-packing companies began to use humane methods of slaughter, but for the most part, animals were killed by the most barbaric methods, with intense suffering. In 1955, when Senator Hubert Humphrey and Representative Martha Griffiths introduced the first humane slaughter bill ever presented to the Congress, the American Meat Institute called it "premature." After all, it was only eighty-two years since Switzerland had passed one, and a mere thirty or forty years behind most other European countries, New Zealand, even the Fiji Islands! Nevertheless, a Congressional committee investigated the slaughterhouses and passed the Humane Slaughter Act of 1958 over the complaints of the meat companies, farmers' organizations, and their friends in the Department of Agriculture. The act requires that animals be stunned before they are shackled and hung upside down by one leg for slaughter.

When the treatment of laboratory animals came to the attention of the federal government in 1965, it was a true breakthrough for groups such as the Animal Welfare

Institute, which had been trying for many years to relieve the plight of the animals sold by dealers to research laboratories. Under the pressure of tremendous public support, Congress passed the Animal Welfare Act of 1967 over the protest of the medical and pharmaceutical industries, as well as those of the dealers that breed and sell animals for sale to laboratories. Animals suffered a setback, though, when the National Society for Medical Research, which represents the interests of sellers and users of lab animals, succeeded in bringing about the laws that exist in most states which require animal shelters to turn over lost and unwanted dogs and cats to laboratories for experimentation.

The Animal Welfare Act states that lab animals must be humanely housed and that pain medication should be used "appropriately." It was strengthened in 1970 and again in 1976, but to this day it specifically covers only a small percentage of the animals used by laboratories. The act also applies to the care of animals in carnivals, circuses, and zoos, and prohibits dogfights. Ironically, it is administered by the Department of Agriculture (which fought the Humane Slaughter Act, remember), and prosecutions or license revocations are rare. The department claims it doesn't have enough agents to enforce the law thoroughly, and even when violations are cited, it takes years of cumbersome litigation before anything is done about them.

Both the Humane Slaughter Act and the Animal Welfare Act represent great triumphs on the part of dedicated people and overwhelming public support, even though these laws have a long way to go in giving the kind of protection most compassionate people feel that animals deserve.

In most states it is against the law to abandon an animal, but people do it every day without fear of being arrested. In some places it is even against the law for a driver to leave an animal hit-and-run on the road—drivers who hit animals are required to stop and help them. Whether or not this law can or will be enforced remains to be seen.

Even with these laws on the books, cruelty and indifference to animals are widespread. This is what is meant by the gap that exists between what the law says and what everybody really believes. Until the majority of people truly believe it is wrong to abandon animals or to drive away without stopping after hitting them on the road, animals' legal rights have very little reality.

Often the protection given to animals by the anticruelty laws applies only to animals that are property. If a hunter shoots a cow, people disapprove and the hunter is punished because he has hurt or killed a piece of property. But if a hunter shoots a deer during the hunting season, and causes it great anguish and death, he isn't thought to be doing anything wrong. In some states, a person can even set a stray cat on fire or otherwise torture it without being punished, because the cat is no one's property.

One problem with enforcing animal protection laws today is that cruelty to animals is often hidden. When carriage horses were beaten, or cattle were driven to exhaustion across the land, or "sports" such as bear baiting were public spectacles, the cruelty was in plain view for everyone to see. Today, animals in puppy mills, research laboratories, factory farms, mink "ranches," or slaughterhouses are behind doors where the public can't see them. Cockfights and dogfights go on in secret places. People who would interfere if they saw a man beating a dog on the street don't know, and don't want to know, what goes on in all the hidden places where animals suffer.

Suppose department stores where fur coats are sold were required to display living animals caught in traps. Suppose supermarkets had anemic veal calves suffering in their cramped, darkened cages for all to see. Suppose drugstores showed animals being subjected to the "writhing test." Would people be so horrified they would put an end to these abuses? Or would we, like the people who perform these cruelties to animals, get used to them and not be bothered after a while?

We have always assumed that human beings are the most intelligent species, but that is because the ways we have devised of measuring intelligence are all human ways. Now, however, we are beginning to discover significant things about the intelligence of other animals, notably, whales, dolphins, and chimpanzees. Persons who argue that the assignment of rights should be based on intelligence soon run into trouble with that line of reasoning. Chimpanzees and gorillas are known to be smarter than many human beings—infants, retarded people, and very old people who have become senile. Also, there are greater differences in intelligence among human beings themselves than there are between human beings and other animals, and there is great variation in intelligence among the other animals. So you can't simply draw a line,

Animal Rights

based on the ability to reason, between human beings and the rest of the animal kingdom.

It's true we are the only animals that have a written language, but that may be because we are the only ones who need one. Other animals communicate perfectly well for their needs. We are not born knowing how to write. If a human being did not know how to write, we would not have the right to trap him, use him for laboratory experiments, or put him in a zoo.

One way to understand how we regard animals in our society is to examine the words we use to describe or refer to them. Animals that hunters prefer are called "game"; those that are spurned by the average hunter are "nongame." Unwanted species of animals that get caught in traps are called "trash," even if it is your pet cat that is trapped instead of a fox or raccoon. The cages in which zoo animals are confined are called "exhibitions." When a small living animal, such as a kitten or rabbit, is tied dangling from a mechanical arm just out of reach of greyhounds that are being taught to race, the animal is simply referred to as the "lure." And any animal that eats other animals is called, often contemptuously, a "predator."

The words used for killing are even more evasive. When a baby seal is clubbed to death, a whale torpedoed, or a deer shot, it is "harvested" as though it were a vegetable. An unwanted pet put to death at an animal shelter is "euthanized" or "put to sleep." In the research laboratory, a dog, monkey, rat, or other animal that is killed in the course of an experiment is "terminated" or "sacrificed."

What can be done to extend the rights of animals? It

is not reasonable to argue that animals should have the same rights as human beings, because they do not need them. For example, an animal doesn't need the right to vote, or to have free schooling. The rights it needs are very modest, really.

Perhaps it should be decided that animals have the right not to be hunted or trapped for anything that human beings have no true need of, such as fur coats. People, having no fur of their own, do need to keep themselves warm in cold weather, but we can no longer claim, as we might have in primitive times, that we need animals' fur for that purpose. As for hunting, very few people must do that to keep from starving—most folks hunt for the pleasure of being outdoors, stalking and killing the animals. How about hunting and catching them with cameras instead? How about doing something else altogether and leaving the animals alone in the few places on earth left for them?

Human beings suffer greatly from diseases and of course we want to discover cures. But now new methods of testing drugs and medical procedures are being developed that are more accurate, quicker, and less expensive than using animals. We now know that experiments done with living animals are often inaccurate anyway. Alternatives are being developed slowly. If the government, which pays for a huge portion of research, announced that it would no longer fund research that used animals, but would grant a lot of money for research on nonanimal substitutes, you can bet that thousands of alternative technologies would be perfected very fast.

Researchers could also be required to pool their

information, to prevent the endless duplication of research that now claims millions of animals. The use of pain killers could be made mandatory, even for mice. And how about ruling out the use of animals for cosmetic research totally? Is it worthwhile to put thousands of animals to painful death each year just to have new shades of lipstick?

The rights of meat animals are more problematical. Most meat animals—chickens, cows, calves, pigs, and lambs—are brought into life through the manipulation of human beings. They are "manufactured" by us, so to speak. They don't exist in the wild, and they are not pets. People regulate their mating and births and their short lives completely. It is unlikely that most people are going to give up eating these animals any time soon, although many compassionate people are vegetarians and the trend toward vegetarianism is growing.

However, if the world's population keeps on growing at its present rate, the time may come when it is no longer practical for us to get our protein through animals. It takes far more edible protein to raise meat animals than it does for us to eat protein directly in its plant state. By processing edible protein through an animal, a great proportion of it is lost. In the not-too-distant future, it may not be possible for us to waste protein for the pleasure of eating meat. Until that time, possibly the only hope for meat animals is to enact stronger humane laws governing the way they are raised, shipped, and slaughtered—and enforce them. We might insist that these beasts have at least the right to be raised and transported comfortably and killed painlessly.

Even more than hunting and trapping, loss of habitat is what has doomed most of the world's wild animals. Environmental scientists estimate that the way things are going, before too many years there just won't be any wilderness left for wild animals to live in. Look at what's happening to the wild elephants in Africa. With uncontrolled human population growth in most of the African countries where elephants live, the pressure for land is pushing them into extinction. The rights of wild animals to their habitats seems to depend on limiting human population growth—and population needs. In our country, population isn't increasing right now, but we go on taking over the wilderness anyway, from building a pipeline in Alaska to constructing huge shopping centers in the countryside.

Do we have the right to keep wild animals in zoos because we like to look at them and study them? Are zoos the only alternative to extinction for wild animals? Animals that are born in zoos live reasonably comfortable lives if they are lucky enough to be in one of the few humane zoos where they have lots of naturalistic space and the companionship of their own kind. Yet even in moderately good zoos, the animals are not safe—they must be protected from vandals, and from zoo directors who sell old animals to hunting ranches.

The rights of pets are different. They are totally dependent on human beings—it is too late in the history of their evolution to grant them freedom as one of their rights. Pets are ready to love us with uncritical loyalty. They need the right to be treated well and cared for lovingly. Sometimes you hear people say they don't believe in

Animal Rights

keeping dogs in cities. Well, dogs have to live where *we* are, and most of the people in the United States live in cities. Furthermore, people need dogs—for companionship, for contact with another creature, for something to love and nurture. Most pet animals are adapted to city living.

Even some people who realize that dogs need people are under the impression that cats can make it on their own. Cats as well as dogs need the right not to be abandoned. Pets also need to be protected from overbreeding. Cats and dogs do not need the right to unlimited reproduction—if they did have it, most of their offspring would be headed for premature death the minute they were born.

It is important for those of us who care about animals to understand what rights they need. The best way to do this is to learn as much as possible about them, and never to lose the ability to put ourselves in their place. It would not be protecting the rights of a seal, a jaguar, or a robin to have it live with us in our house, no matter how much love we gave it. It would not be appropriate for the rights of a cow or dog to turn it loose in the mountains, no matter how much it likes to wander. It would be cruel to take all the zoo animals and simply turn them loose—even if their survival instincts were intact, there are not enough safe natural habitats left for them.

So far, our record has not been good. Since animals can't speak for themselves, their rights must be defended by people who speak for them. The courts will take the rights of animals seriously only when we, the people, decide to take animal rights seriously in our daily lives.

Further Reading

Adams, Richard. *The Plague Dogs.* New York: Alfred A. Knopf, 1977. Paperback—New York: Fawcett World Library, 1978.
  Powerful novel about two laboratory dogs who escape and live in the wild with a fox.

Amory, Cleveland. *Man Kind?: Our Incredible War on Wildlife.* New York: Harper & Row, 1974. Paperback—New York: Dell Publishing Co., 1975.
  A humane activist speaks against hunting and trapping.

Batten, Peter. *Living Trophies.* New York: Thomas Y. Crowell Co., 1976.
  An exposé of U.S. zoos by a former zoo director and humane activist.

Caras, Roger. *Dangerous to Man.* New York: Holt, Rinehart & Winston, 1975.
  Myths about wildlife; separates fact from hearsay and superstition about animal nature and behavior.

Carson, Gerald. *Men, Beasts and Gods: A History of Cruelty and Kindness to Animals.* New York: Charles Scribner's Sons, 1972.
  Thoughtful review of our treatment of animals.

Cousteau, Jacques-Yves, and Diolé, Philippe. *The Whale: Mighty Monarch of the Sea.* New York: Doubleday & Co., 1972. Paperback—New York: A & W Publishers, 1977.
  ———. *Dolphins.* New York: Doubleday & Co., 1975.
  Adventures and photographs by the great underwater explorer.

Curtis, Patricia. *Animal Doctors.* New York: Delacorte Press, 1972.
  What it is like to be a veterinarian and how to become one.

Further Reading

Domalain, Jean-Yves. *The Animal Connection: The Confessions of an Ex-Wild Animal Trafficker.* New York: William Morrow & Co., 1977.
An exposé by a former wild animal collector who tells his story of the capture and sale of exotic pets for zoos and trade.

Donovan, John. *Family.* New York: Harper & Row, 1976.
Fiction; the story of a group of apes who escape from a laboratory.

Durrell, Gerald. *The Stationary Ark.* New York: Simon & Schuster, 1976.
The famous writer about animals tells about his efforts to create a perfect zoo on the island of Jersey.

Fox, Michael. *Between Animal and Man.* New York: Coward, McCann & Geoghegan, 1976.
Animal behavior and relationships with people, by a veterinarian active in humane work.

Fox, Michael, and Morris, Richard Knowles. *On the Fifth Day.* Washington, D.C.: Acropolis Books, 1978.
Essays on animal rights and human ethics.

Godlovitch, Roslind; Godlovitch, Stanley; and Harris, John, eds. *Animals, Men and Morals.* New York: Taplinger Publishing Co., 1972.
Essays on the mistreatment of nonhumans.

Hodge, Guy R. *Careers Working with Animals.* Washington, D.C.: Acropolis Books Ltd., 1979.
Informative roundup of occupational opportunities in animal welfare, conservation, environmental protection, and allied professions.

Kevles, Bettyann. *Watching the Wild Apes.* New York: E.P. Dutton & Co., 1976.
The natural behavior of chimpanzees, gorillas, and orangutans.

Lappé, Frances Moore. *Diet for a Small Planet.* New York: Ballantine Books, 1975.
   The advantages of meatless nutrition; with recipes.
Leavitt, Emily Stewart. *Animals and Their Legal Rights.* Washington, D.C.: Animal Welfare Institute, 1978.
   History and facts of animal protection legislation.
Lopez, Barry Holstun. *Of Wolves and Men.* New York: Charles Scribner's Sons, 1978.
   Human beings' fascination with wolves through the ages, and our destruction of them.
Mason, Jim, and Singer, Peter. *Animal Factories.* New York: Crown Publishers, 1980.
   The realities of modern factory farming.
McIntyre, Joan, ed. *Mind in the Waters.* New York: Charles Scribner's Sons, 1974.
   Writings about whales and dolphins.
Morse, Mel. *Ordeal of the Animals.* Englewood Cliffs, N.J.: Prentice-Hall, 1968.
   An overview of cruelty to animals in all areas: pets, wildlife, entertainment, laboratory research, raising and slaughter for food.
Pratt, Dallas. *Painful Experiments on Animals—and the Alternatives.* New York: Argus Archives, 1979.
   A humane scientist reviews laboratory animal experiments that cause suffering, the ethical questions involved, and alternatives.
Redding, William, and Stewart, Jean. *Traps and Trapping, Furs and Fashion.* New York: Argus Archives, 1977.
   Informative overview of the slaughter of wild furbearers.
Regan, Tom, and Singer, Peter, eds. *Animal Rights and Human Obligations.* Englewood Cliffs, N.J.: Prentice-Hall, 1976.

Further Reading

Essays on our relationship to animals and our practice of destroying them for food and experimentation.

Regenstein, Lewis. *The Politics of Extinction.* New York: Macmillan, 1975.
Behind-the-scenes exposé of the extermination of wildlife.

Ryden, Hope. *America's Last Wild Horses.* New York: E.P. Dutton & Co., 1978.
A respected wildlife defender examines the plight of the mustangs.

———. *God's Dog.* New York: Penguin Books, 1979.
A celebration of the much-misunderstood North American coyote.

Singer, Peter. *Animal Liberation.* New York: New York Review, 1975. Paperback—New York: Avon Books, 1975.
Revealing philosophical and practical examination of our use of animals for laboratory research and the way we raise them for food.

Tuttle, Margaret Wheaton. *The Crimson Cage.* Martha's Vineyard, Mass.: Tashmoo Press, 1978.
Realistic novel about a family pet that is kidnapped and used by an experimental laboratory. Strong stuff but deserves to be read. Proceeds from book go to a spay/neuter clinic.

Weber, William J. *Wild Orphan Babies: Caring for Them, Setting Them Free.* New York: Holt, Rinehart & Winston, 1978.
A veterinarian tells how to save orphaned wild mammals and birds.

Outstanding Animal Magazines

Animals
Bimonthly publication for the Massachusetts Society for the Prevention of Cruelty to Animals, 350 South Huntington Ave., Boston, Mass. 02130

Defenders
Bimonthly publication of Defenders of Wildlife organization.

The Humane Society News
Quarterly magazine of the Humane Society of the United States.

Mainstream
Quarterly publication of Animal Protection Institute.

Pet News
Bimonthly educational pet journal, 44 Court St., Brooklyn, N.Y. 11201

National Humane Organizations That Work to Help Animals

Here are some of the national societies that are involved in major areas of animal protection. This is not to deny the fine work of the many, many local groups that also deserve support and participation.

American Horse Protection Association
   1312 18 St. N.W., Washington, D.C. 20036
   Investigates and protests abuses of all horses; the only national humane organization dedicated to the welfare of horses, both wild and domestic. Publishes newsletter. Has junior division.

American Society for the Prevention of Cruelty to Animals
   441 E. 92 St., New York, N.Y. 10028
   Oldest and largest humane shelter society in U.S. Publishes information on national humane issues, pet care, pet shelters, spay/neutering. Investigates and prosecutes cruelty cases in New York State. Has shelters and hospitals. Quarterly bulletin.

Animal Protection Institute
   P.O. Box 22505, Sacramento, Calif. 95822
   Works to end cruelty to pets, domestic livestock, wildlife. Conducts humane education. Publishes quarterly magazine, *Mainstream*.

Animal Welfare Institute
   P.O. Box 3650, Washington, D.C. 20007
   Educational organization that investigates and works to alleviate suffering of laboratory animals, factory farm animals, wildlife, endangered species (especially whales and dolphins). Publishes reference books, quarterly information report.

Beauty Without Cruelty
175 W. 12 St., New York, N.Y. 10011
Conducts research and publishes information on cruelty of trapping and laboratory research. Separate branch of organization makes and sells cosmetics that are not tested on animals; also imitation fur coats and jackets.

Canadian Federation of Humane Societies
101 Champagne Ave.
Ottawa K1S 4P3, Ontario
Large humane association with many different member organizations that work to reduce suffering of laboratory animals, pets, animals raised for meat.

The Cousteau Society
Box 2002, New York, N.Y. 10017
Environmental protection and research organization whose purpose is to explore and defend the life that exists in the oceans. Publishes newsletter.

Defenders of Wildlife
1244 19 St., N.W., Washington, D.C. 20036
Educational group for wildlife protection. Publishes bimonthly magazine, *Defenders*. Has junior division.

Friends of Animals
11 W. 60 St., New York, N.Y. 10023
Works to abolish hunting and trapping of wildlife; protect sea animals; end abuses of laboratory animals, food animals, and animals used for entertainment; control pet overpopulation. Emphasizes activism. Welcomes young adult members.

The Fund for Animals
140 W. 57 St., New York, N.Y. 10019
Activist and educational organization for protection and defense of all animals—especially wildlife, sea animals, animals used for entertainment. Publishes newsletter.

National Humane Organizations 147

Greenpeace
240 Fort Mason, San Francisco, Calif. 94123
Activist ecology group campaigns to protect seals, whales, dolphins through direct nonviolent intervention.

Humane Information Services
4495 Ninth Ave N., St. Petersburg, Fla. 33713
Conducts investigations and research, publishes informative *Report to Humanitarians* newsletter of facts and analyses of humane problems.

The Humane Society of the United States
2100 L St., N.W., Washington, D.C. 20037
Activist and educational organization for animal defense and protection in all areas. Has educational division; youth division. Publishes quarterly magazine, *Humane Society News*; also magazine for very young children, *Kind*. Has research division, The Institute for the Study of Animal Problems.

International Primate Protection League
P.O. Box 9086, Berkeley, Calif. 94709
Works to prevent, expose, and end cruelty to apes and monkeys in laboratories and exhibitions. Publishes newsletter.

National Cat Protection Society
340 W. Willow St., P.O. Box 6065,
Long Beach, Calif. 90806
Educational society on behalf of cats. Publishes *Voice of the Voiceless*, and *Feline Defenders*. Conducts rescue work; has shelters.

Society for Animal Rights
421 S. State St., Clarks Summit, Pa. 18411
Activist and educational organization; furnishes information on rights of animals and violations of those rights. Publishes newsletter.

United Action for Animals
205 E. 42 St., New York, N.Y. 10017
Works to encourage the development and use of advanced technology to replace the use of living animals in laboratory experimentation. Publishes newsletter.

Vegetarian Information Service
Box 5888, Washington, D.C. 20014
Promotes health and nutritional benefits of vegetarian diets, news of vegetarian movement. Publishes leaflets, newsletter.

Wildlife Preservation Trust, International
34th and Girard Streets, Philadelphia, Pa. 19104
Educational and fundraising organization founded by Gerald Durrell to support captive breeding of endangered species, including work at Mr. Durrell's zoo on the island of Jersey in the English Channel. Has newsletter and informative annual journal.